THE PRESS CLUB

MODERN GREEK COOKERY

THE PRESS CLUß

MODERN GREEK COOKERY

GEORGE CALOMBARIS

PHOTOGRAPHY DEAN CAMBRAY

NEW HOLLAND

I DEDICATE THIS BOOK TO MY GRANDFATHER:
GEORGE DIMITRIOS CALOMBARIS (1912–1975)

'I HAVE NEVER MET YOU,
BUT I AM SURE I WILL MEET YOU ONE DAY.'
LOVE GEORGE

First published in Australia in 2008 by
New Holland Publishers (Australia) Pty Ltd
Sydney • Auckland • London • Cape Town

1/66 Gibbes Street Chatswood NSW 2067 Australia
218 Lake Road Northcote Auckland New Zealand
86 Edgware Road London W2 2EA United Kingdom
80 McKenzie Street Cape Town 8001 South Africa

A record of this book is held at the National Library of Australia

ISBN 9781741105810

Publisher: Fiona Schultz
Editor: Kay Proos
Managing Editor: Lliane Clarke
Designer: Tania Gomes
Photography: Dean Cambray
Production Assistant: Liz Malcolm
Production Manager: Linda Bottari
Printer: Toppan Printing Co (China)

10 9 8 7 6 5 4 3 2 1

THE PRESS CLUB RESTAURANT AND BAR

72 Flinders St, Melbourne Vic 3000
Telephone: 61 (3) 9677 9677
www.thepressclub.com.au

ACKNOWLEDGEMENTS

Firstly, I would like to thank my family for bringing the culture, values and passion from the motherland. Thanks Dad and Mum!

'The qualities of exceptional chefs are those akin to a successful tightrope walker, to always go out on a limb.' In a nutshell this sums up my kitchen at The Press Club. Starting with Head Chef Justin Wise, Travis McAuley, Ian Burch, Maria Klinakis, Petros Dellidis, Theo Paraskevas and the entire kitchen team. You guys are my sanity—thank you for your inspiration and loyalty.

The rest: I'd like to thank the maestro, the one that makes it happen everyday Angie Giannakodakis and her support team, Andrew Phillpot, Trish Mortenson, Aidan Raftery, Olivia Hardie, Lauren Calleja, Malcolm Singh and all of the waiters and bartenders that work every day to complete The Press Club experience.

These three guys, with their three different characters, have successfully supported and believed in my dream—Tony Lachimea, George Sykiotis and Joe Calleja. I thank them for their inspiration and motivation. All are tireless in their passion for The Press Club in their own ways.

I would like to make a special mention to Buro Architects, Anne from Anne Angel Designs and Grant and the team from .commedia.

Without my suppliers I would not be able to produce the food. They are thankless in the job that they do and vital to the day-to-day running of The Press Club and have been supporting us since we have opened our doors. San Pellegrino, Moffat, Chefs Hat, Bills Farm, Campania, Chef's Choice, Elco Foods, Frankies, French par bake, Imports of France, Largo Butchers, Ocean Made Seafoods, Poseidon Seafoods, Sweet Sunflower, The Golden Olive, The Saffron Gatherer, Tip Top Poultry, Cuisine Boards and Village Cheese. Many thanks for your continued support and relationships.

Most importantly, I would like to thank Dean Cambray for bringing The Press Club to life with his fantastic photography. It's great to work with a photographer who actually understands food.

CONTENTS

FOREWORD

After living in Greece for over a decade, I decided to come back home to Melbourne a little wiser and a lot more humble. I came back wanting to show what real Greek restaurants are and what real Greeks are like, after all to be Greek is a state of mind rather than a nationality. It's been a long journey since but really it only started with a phone call to George. I called him and asked him if he was still looking for a restaurant manager and he was, 'I'm a restaurant manager, I'm available and I'm Greek', he laughed and we made a time to meet. That was the best phone call I made. At The Press Club he is the driving force and the passionate young man in front and behind the pass. He has been a relentless believer in good modern Hellenic food and his perseverance has paid off.

As Hellenes, George has made us all proud.

Angie Giannakodakis, Restaurant Manager

Well it all started nearly five years ago at a restaurant named 'Reserve'. I still remember my trial day. I was so nervous, nothing was going right. Burning nearly everything, but still George gave me the chance to work for him.

I wanted to work for George because he always looks outside the box, with extremely high expectations.

Reserve closed suddenly and the idea of The Press Club started. What George described to me back then had me excited and I knew I wanted to be involved. I have been with George all this time, and I can definitely say that it has been the best period of my life. I have achieved so many career goals so far.

I look forward to coming to work everyday, although the hours are long and hard, we are one big family here and we all work hard together to achieve the one result.

The Press Club to me is about the customer. Forget the egotistic chef or the pompous waiter; it's about giving the customer an experience, based on family cultures, and yes, Greek food!

Justin Wise, Head Chef

INTRODUCTION

There is nothing better in a chef's career than to cook food for family and friends. I have been cooking for ten years and it feels like I have only just begun. I can't tell you that my life to date has been tough. I have had a great journey. I come from a big 'wog' family where the values of life are its number-one priority. Well, up there with food of course.

When I was growing up food was cultural and religious. I believe if you blindfolded me, turned off time, then turned it back on and walked me into my 'yia yia's' (grandmother's) house, I could tell you what time of the year it was through all the cooking aromas.

I get this question all the time, 'Why did you become a chef?' I don't know. I love it. You have to. No one works 18 hours a day for a laugh. I was no good at school. My parents sent me to a private boys' college that was one big party at the weekends; I washed pots and pans at a mediocre pasta restaurant. I still remember as I was washing the frying pans, I'd look at the chefs cooking and dream that I would get out there one day and wear a big tall hat too. The chef would get me to make the garden salads up before every service. He would tell me, 'George, make the cucumber slices stand up like aeroplane wings'. At that point I thought I was a chef. What a joke.

I finished Year 12 and got an apprenticeship at the Hotel Sofitel, which included the three-hatted 'Le Restaurant'. What an experience. Out of 11 first-year apprentices, only two remained by the end of our first year. Raymond Capaldi was the chef for my first two years there. He was a tough taskmaster. Raymond created a 'chef cult', a kitchen full of passionate individuals. Those who weren't passionate were out the door. I worked hard. I wanted to get into 'Le Restaurant'. After two years of hard graft and long hours I got there. At this point I was learning all the basics: stocks, sauces, vegetable preparation etc. Priceless learning. I was a sponge. I learnt techniques that I still enforce at The Press Club today. We don't have recipes at The Press Club, we have guidelines and techniques. We cook from the heart. The minute it becomes a job, then quit. Become a tram driver. There is nothing worse in life than a bad dining experience. For example, take the staff dinner at The Press Club. It's the job of the apprentice and it must be good. I believe if the staff don't eat well, then how do our customers?

Well, my time at Sofitel had finally come to an end and I decided to move on with Raymond and Gary Meghian—Ray's business partner who was the executive sous-chef at Sofitel—to their new restaurant, café, produce store, and event centre. What a learning curve. From Commis I became Head Chef in six months. Fenix was amazing; Ray and Gary let me bring out my own style there. I learnt a lot from those two men; I took the good and learnt from the bad. Ray taught me how to think about food and become a visionary; Gary taught me how to be a manager. He always said to me, 'people have good and bad aspects'. So I have learnt to find the good and build on it. My kitchen at The Press Club is made up of artists, grafters and donkeys. Why? Because I have been all of them. They are all treated equally with respect. Some days I have to be all of them again.

I still remember serving my first special, 'Seared Scallops, Chicken and Madeira Parfait with White Grape Vinaigrette'. Donovan Cooke (former chef of EST EST EST) was in for lunch that day and ate it. He loved it. I don't serve that dish now, it's not Greek, but I still use the techniques. The scallops are cooked the same way. Seared golden-brown on one side, seasoned with salt and served immediately while they are still opaque in the middle. While we are on the topic of salt, let me continue; salt is seasoning, pepper is not. This is the problem with chefs, they follow and copy too much; they don't think about the product. Pepper is a spice. We rarely cook with pepper at The Press Club, and I also ban waiters from wandering around the restaurant with pepper mills, poking them at people like some sort of ancient ritual. We season all our food with salt and also provide Cyprian Black Sea Salt on each table. Why? Because some customers like more salt, just like some customers like their meat well done. We allow it and serve it to please the customer.

I have travelled a lot through my cooking: Singapore, China, India, Italy, Greece and let's not forget the UK. I did unpaid work at a two-star Michelin Restaurant. It was a kitchen full of egos. I hate egocentric chefs. They don't belong in my kitchen. I guess that's why that restaurant closed down six months later.

My next stop was Reserve Restaurant at Federation Square. My first lone gig. As a chef de cuisine. What a roller coaster! At 24 years of age I won Young Chef of the Year as well as Best New Restaurant and two Chefs Hats. We had a very busy first year. I was cooking food for my ego, food beyond Melbourne's time, masked as 'molecular gastronomy'. We had customers fly in from all over the world to try it. Every chef would come and check it out, some loving it, some stealing ideas and some slandering it. I understood I would be open to criticism as I was cooking controversial food.

I learnt a hell of a lot at Reserve about how not to run a business. The key to a successful business is to surround yourself with good people. That's the whole foundation of The Press Club. Everyone, from my business partners to my kitchen hands, all have the direction, the vision and each of us has jobs to do to a high standard. I have to lead by example, because I am the head and I never want it to fail. I owe it to the men and women in my team, I give 100 per cent to each and every one.

You know what I hated about Reserve? Some customers would come in frequently, and want to see me. How dare I take a day off? F--k! Does Valentino sew all the buttons on his suits? I don't think so. My creative soul grows when I am not in the kitchen. My style has matured. I am now on the right path. My food has soul now; before it lacked substance. Yes, I have had great publicity. Why? Because I am honest with the critics. There's no bullshit. They're human too. I don't tweak dishes up when they come into my restaurant. Nor do I panic. We just get on with the job. I address them like I address my family. I want people to come in and experience what the Greeks do well . . . the generosity of the spirit.

I still remember as a child I was so embarrassed about being a Greek-Australian. None of my friends were Greeks. It was so not cool. At home we ate Greek-Cypriot Food (my mother being Cypriot); we drank Greek Coffee (not Turkish!); we spoke Greek; we went to the Greek Club for dinner-dances. Everything we did was Greek. As painful as I thought it was back then, I long for it now. I am proud to be a Greek-Australian and honoured to have the first Modern Greek Restaurant in Melbourne.

2004 was a big year for being Greek or having Greek heritage. It was the year when Greece won the European Football Cup, the European Basket Ball Tournament and convinced the world of its prowess with an outstanding Olympic Games. Through this, my vision for The Press Club evolved. My passion for all things Greek appeared. I honour my parents, grandparents and all those Greeks who came to Australia in the 1950s and helped build a country with such culture. Melbourne has the largest Greek population of any city outside Athens, but not one restaurant that we could put on the world stage of 'top restaurant'. So, the birth of The Press Club Restaurant and Bar began. A modern agora (meeting place) for exceptional modern Greek food, wine and service. My food is feminine in many ways. I believe that the female is the most beautiful creature in the world. I always have a woman in my kitchen. Good kitchens are made of different characters. Two of the same are dangerous. And no, I am not sexist. All I want is the best result for my customers. Testosterone is the Achilles' heel of a male chef. It is calming to have a female presence.

The food at The Press Club is my interpretation of Greek Cuisine. It has soul, elegance, substance, technique and above all, respect and understanding of the product. People's perception of Greek cuisine is dips and fried cheese. Unfortunately, that's not Greek, that's tourist island food. I have no signature dishes, they all have a story and by the time you cook them I will have changed them, tweaked them, developed them. I don't sit still. I am not a passenger. No dish is perfect, nor have I invented any of them. A chef who says he has invented a dish is a bullshit artist. The closest dish I have nearly come to perfection with is the Natural Oysters spiked with Attiki Honey and Almond Dressing. It's so feminine and so natural. I stole the dressing idea from my mate David Tsirekas from Perama Restaurant in Sydney (thanks Dave). I learnt how to shuck oysters as an apprentice. You never wash the oyster; you leave it in its own juices. You wouldn't wash a piece of beef under the tap.

Enjoy the Press Club dishes and remember, recipes are not set in stone, they're guidelines. Cooking comes from the heart. Think from there when you cook, and enjoy!

Kali Orexi

George Calombaris

ΟΙΝΟΠΟΙΗΤΙΚΗ
ΣΥΝΕΤΑΙΡΙΣΜΟΣ
ΤΥΡΝΑΒΟΥ

OUZO

παράδοση   παραγωγή
όχι μόνο στην Ελλάδα,
...τον Τύρναβο το έκανε ξα-
...σε όλο τον κόσμο.
...ο Αγροτικός Οινοποιητι-
...Συνεταιρισμός Τυρνάβου συνεχίζει
...την παράδοση με την βοήθεια
...σύγχρονης τεχνολογίας και με τη
...κλειστικά αμπελουργικής...

COOPERATIVE WINE
PURE - NATURAL

OUZO –
THE HELLENIC NATIONAL DRINK

There's an image of Greece that has been planted in my mind for many years now. In a dream sequence, I'm back in my local platia (square) on a warm summer night surrounded by friends. We sit on wooden and straw chairs at a small round table eating pikilia of mezedes and slowly drinking ouzo we call the *'elixir of life'* with ice clinking in the glass.

The euphoria of that moment comes back to me whenever there is a small bottle of ouzo and cheeky little appetisers we call mezedes laid out.

With nostalgia in our hearts, The Press Club's grand selection of small dishes, such as octopus, whitebait, dolmades, toursi, anchovies and a whole procession of meze, complement all styles of ouzo.

Every region of Greece has its own special blend of ouzo which is determined by the grapes that are used and the herbs and spices available. Our favourites lie in the main ouzo-producing area of Lesvos or Mitilini. The island uses Lisbori aniseed with a touch of mastic and island herbs and spices from the neighbouring island of Chios. For robust, masculine aromas we turn to the traditional Piraeus based ouzo whose flavours are inspired by the Greek diaspora of Asia Minor. The mainland ouzo from the Peloponnese, Thessaly and Macedonia all have distinct characteristics but more so when diluted with water. The flavours vary from more alpine aromas to lighter fennel or spice aromas thanks to the ever zealous ouzo makers.

The serving of ouzo is such a sensitive matter that we accompany it with a small bottle of still mineral water, cubes of ice and a little dish of something savoury or fatty. Tasting an ouzo straight allows you to see what strength you need to dilute it to once the food arrives. Experiences vary and the secret to a safer experience is to wisely acknowledge the natural pairing of the food connection. Try marinated or char-grilled octopus with the first pouring of Plomari ouzo and you are in Hellenic heaven. Ask for an ouzo and cola and you'll get them served separately. A ritual can't be spoilt.

Stin igia mas! To our health!

THE PRESS CLUB

A Journey with Food

Mezedes—Appetisers

Orektika—Small dishes

KYRIA—MAIN DISHES

SYNOTHEFTIKA—SIDE DISHES

GLYKA—SWEET DISHES

STANDARD RECIPES

MEZEDES
Appetisers

'A SMILING WAITER APPROACHES THE TABLE
WITH A LONG WOODEN BOARD SCATTERED WITH
CHEEKY, TANTALISING MORSELS OF DIFFERENT
COLOURS, TEXTURES AND FLAVOURS.'

MEZEDES—APPETISERS

A smiling waiter approaches the table with a long wooden board scattered with cheeky, tantalising morsels of different colours, textures and flavours. As the board is placed upon the table, conversation stops for a moment to hear the names of these bite-sized delicacies: Saganaki Martini; Toursi; Crispy Fried School Prawns with Ouzo Mayonnaise; Thyme Marinated Octopus; Oysters with Ouzo and Shallot Dressing . . . eyes light up and mouths begin to water. The waiter leaves, forks dig into the dishes, ouzo glasses are lifted and the conversation begins to flow again.

Mezedes are small dishes that tease the palate whilst the diner waits for the next course, or they can become a whole meal in themselves. They are to be enjoyed slowly, amongst a group of friends and family, accompanied with some ouzo whilst the conversation and laughter flow.

Mezedes are not simply an array of different dishes, rather they are about creating a balance of flavours and textures amongst the selection of dishes presented. There will be something crunchy, something refreshing, something salty and something sweet. At The Press Club this balance can be found on our mezedes board. However, even if you choose just one of our mezedes, it's the ideal way to awaken the palate. The Saganaki Martini for example, a transparent liquid of a tomato infusion spiked with gin, finely diced tomatoes, cucumbers, chives and candied Kalamata olives that float amongst the liquid, all topped with a haloumi skewer resting across the glass. A perfect way to experience true mezedes is at your local mezedopolio, a place that serves only meze. Every Sunday lunch, customers at The Press Club can enjoy a masa menu, where the restaurant turns into a vibrant place full of people enjoying a long, slow lunch of mezedes, local wine and ouzo.

SAGANAKI MARTINI

Serves 4

This dish represents The Press Club; innovation, tradition and intense flavour. The perception of the saganaki is that it's the name given to the fried cheese, unfortunately this isn't the case as saganaki comes from the name of the special frying pan that fish is cooked in. Once cooked, the Greeks would remove the fish and cook the cheese and bread to soak up the fishy flavours left in the pan. Be warned that the olives take a long time in the oven. You can make them weeks in advance and store them in an airtight container in the refrigerator until needed.

200G (6½OZ) KALAMATA BLACK OLIVES

1 TABLESPOON CASTER SUGAR

200G (6½OZ) HALOUMI CHEESE

4 HALOUMI SKEWERS

50G (2OZ) TOMATO

20G (¾OZ) CUCUMBER

1 TABLESPOON CHIVES

¾ CUP (190ML/6FL OZ) TOMATO GIN TEA (SEE TOMATO GIN TEA RECIPE)

RED KAHEL TO GARNISH

1. Remove seeds from olives and finely dice. Place on a flat tray lined with greaseproof paper. Lightly dust with the sugar and place in a very low oven, 80°C (175°F), Gas Mark ½ for 12 hours.
2. Cut haloumi into 1cm (2.5in) squares and thread 3 cubes onto each skewer.
3. Blanch tomatoes in boiling water for 10 seconds, remove, then immediately refresh in iced water. Peel them with a small knife. Quarter the tomatoes then remove seeds and cut flesh into 2mm x 2mm (¹/₁₀in x ¹/₁₀in) squares. Set aside.
4. Peel cucumber then cut in quarters lengthways, remove seeds then dice into 2mm x 2mm (¹/₁₀in ¹/₁₀in) squares. Set aside.
5. Finely slice chives.
6. Place tomato, cucumber, candied olives and chopped chives into a bowl, mix well and divide evenly into the bottom of 4 Martini glasses.
7. Fill each Martini glass three-quarters full with the tomato gin tea, and garnish with red kahel.
8. In a frying pan, fry haloumi skewers until golden brown on each side.
9. Place 1 skewer over each glass and serve.

Tomato Gin Tea
Serves 4 (Makes 1 litre)

Please note that this needs straining overnight.

¼ CUP (60ML/2FL OZ) PAPER COFFEE-BAG FILTER (SEE NOTES)

1KG (2LB) OVER-RIPE TOMATOES

10 BASIL LEAVES

½ SMALL RED ONION, PEELED

1 GARLIC CLOVE

20ML (¾FL OZ) WORCESTERSHIRE SAUCE

5 DROPS TABASCO SAUCE

¼ CUP (60ML/2FL OZ) GIN

1. Place filter bag inside a colander placed over a bucket (see Notes).
2. Place all ingredients, except gin, into the blender and blend for 1 minute, or until completely smooth.
3. Pour blended liquid into filter bag and allow to strain overnight.
4. Discard pulp and filter bag and add gin to remaining liquid, to serve.

CHEF'S NOTE: You can use either an oil or coffee paper filter bag. I use a chinois—mesh-in my kitchen, which is a conical mesh strainer with one handle; if you don't have one you can use a colander lined with a clean chux cloth (J cloth/everyday cleaning towel).

Mezedes

Natural Oysters Spiked with Attiki Honey and Almond Dressing

Serves 4

This dish is both feminine and sensual. The oysters must be shucked to order and the honey must be Attiki, a true representation of great Greek produce.

12 NATURAL OYSTERS, SHUCKED (SEE NOTE)

⅙ CUP (40ML/1½FL OZ) ATTIKI HONEY AND ALMOND DRESSING (SEE ATTIKI HONEY AND ALMOND DRESSING RECIPE)

FRESH LEMON, TO GARNISH

CYPRUS BLACK SEA SALT, TO GARNISH

1. Lay oysters on a large serving plate.
2. Spoon honey and almond dressing over oysters, and serve with fresh lemon and Cyprus black sea salt.

CHEF'S NOTE: For good oysters ask your fishmonger to shuck the oysters but leave the lids on as this will prevent the oysters from drying out, as well as keeping all their natural juices inside. Never wash the oysters in water as you will dilute their flavour by doing this.

Mezedes

ATTIKI HONEY AND ALMOND DRESSING

Serves 4 (Makes 300ml)

¾ CUP (190ML/6FL OZ) ATTIKI HONEY

¾ TABLESPOON FISH SAUCE

2 LIMES

10 FRESH CORIANDER (CILANTRO) LEAVES

50G (2OZ) ALMONDS (SLICED)

1. Place honey in a pan and gently heat until it becomes runny.
2. Remove from heat and add fish sauce, the juice of 1 lime and the zest of 2 limes.
3. Allow to stand for 1 hour.
4. Finely slice coriander leaves.
5. Toast almonds lightly in a preheated cool–warm oven, 160°C (310°F) Gas Mark 2½ until golden brown.
6. Add coriander and almonds to the honey dressing and serve.

'ALL MY CHEFS WEAR SHORT SLEEVED JACKETS. WHY? BECAUSE THEY RESPECT THEIR MOST IMPORTANT PIECE OF COOKING EQUIPMENT—THE STOVE. FROM THERE THEY RESPECT THE FOOD. ABOVE ALL, THEY RESPECT THEMSELVES.'
GEORGE CALOMBARIS

Black Mussels
Stuffed with Rabbit Baklava

Serves 4

This dish represents the Greek Islands and the mainland. I call it 'land and sea'. The saltiness of the black mussels (make sure they're live), with the sweet, delicate rabbit baklava is an outstanding combination. Don't forget to tell your diner to remove the twine before eating!

1KG (2LB) BLACK MUSSELS (CLAMS)

4 SMALL GOLDEN SHALLOTS

GARLIC CLOVE, HALVED

⅙ CUP (40ML/1½FL OZ) OLIVE OIL

½ CUP (125ML/4FL OZ) WHITE WINE

¾ CUP (190ML/6FL OZ) CHICKEN STOCK (SEE CHICKEN STOCK STANDARD RECIPE)

200G (6½OZ) RABBIT BAKLAVA (SEE RABBIT BAKLAVA RECIPE)

COOK'S TWINE – APPROX 20CM PER MUSSEL

100G (3½OZ) CHICKPEAS (COOKED OR CANNED)

4 WHITE ANCHOVY FILLETS

50G (2OZ) BUTTER

CHICKPEA CRESS, TO SERVE

1. Clean and debeard mussels (see Notes).
2. Roughly slice shallots and garlic.
3. Heat oil in a heavy based saucepan until hot. Add the mussels and leave for 30 seconds.
4. Then add shallots, garlic, wine and stock. Cover the saucepan and cook for a further 3 minutes, or until the mussels open. Discard any unopened mussels.
5. Remove pan from heat and and strain through a colander into a bowl, reserving stock.
6. Place cling film over colander, ensuring mussels and stock are well covered and allow to cool for 1 hour in the fridge.

7. Place 1 tablespoon of the Rabbit Baklava mix into each mussel. Close the shells together by using cook's twine and tie tightly.

8. To serve, preheat oven to hot, 200°C (400°F) Gas Mark 6 and place mussels into a pan along with mussel stock and bake for 5 minutes.

9. Remove from oven and place mussels onto a serving plate, reserving the mussel stock.

10. Heat stock to simmering point and add the chickpeas and anchovies.

11. Add butter and season to taste (see Notes).

12. Pour stock over mussels and garnish with red kahel, to serve.

CHEF'S NOTE: A mussel's beard is its umbilical cord during its growth in the sea. It uses it to attach itself to its farming post. This beard must be removed (to 'debeard') simply by pulling it out of its shell before cooking.

Adding butter or oil to a sauce (to monte) enriches it and results in a velvety and smooth sauce.

Rabbit Baklava

Serves 4

Vegetable oil, to fry

4 rabbit legs

1 carrot, diced

½ celery stick, diced

½ brown onion, diced

3 garlic cloves, sliced

½ cup (125ml/4fl oz) white wine

¼ cup (60ml/2fl oz) sherry vinegar

12 cups (3l/4¾pt) chicken stock (see Chicken Stock standard recipe)

1 tablespoon thyme

30g (1oz) walnuts

30g (1oz) almonds

4 peppercorns

2 bay leaves

½ bunch chives

4 sprigs parsley

¼ cup fresh breadcrumbs

⅔ cup (160ml/5fl oz) Attiki honey

1. To make the rabbit braise, preheat oven to 160°C (310°F) Gas Mark 2.
2. Add oil to a saucepan and seal the rabbit legs until golden brown. Remove legs from pan and place in a deep baking dish.
4. Add thyme, carrot, celery, onion and garlic to the saucepan and cook until golden brown.
5. Deglaze the pan with the wine and vinegar (see Note). Add chicken stock, peppercorns and bay leaves to the pan and let simmer. Remove from heat and add cooked vegetables to the rabbit legs.
8. Cover baking dish with foil and place in the preheated oven for 2½ hours.
9. Remove rabbit legs from dish and take off all the meat and shred. Place shredded meat in a bowl and set aside.
11. Strain stock through a fine colander, return stock to the saucepan and reduce by half.
13. Add enough sauce to the shredded rabbit to bind.
14. Pan fry walnuts and almonds until golden brown. Then add walnuts, almonds, chopped chives and parsley, breadcrumbs and honey to the rabbit. Add salt, to taste.

Chef's Note: To deglaze means to add liquid to a hot pan or baking dish to lift all of the cooking flavours from the bottom of the pan.

'THIS DISH REPRESENTS THE GREEK
ISLANDS AND THE MAINLAND.
I CALL IT LAND AND SEA'.
GEORGE CALOMBARIS

Lamb and Olive Lady's Fingers, Beetroot Tzatziki

Serves 4

This dish reminds me of my childhood, when my 'yia yia' would give them to us as a little snack. She put cinnamon in her recipe and you can too, if you want.

½ ONION

1 GARLIC CLOVE

VEGETABLE OIL, TO FRY

200G (7OZ) LAMB MINCE (GROUND LAMB)

¼ CUP (60ML/2FL OZ) MADEIRA

1 PINCH SALT

½ CUP (125ML/4FL OZ) CHICKEN STOCK (SEE CHICKEN STOCK STANDARD RECIPE)

30G (1OZ) GREEN OLIVES

100G (3½OZ) BUTTER

4 SHEETS FILO PASTRY

1 TABLESPOON ICING SUGAR, TO SERVE

4 PORTIONS OF BEETROOT TZATZIKI (SEE BEETROOT TZATZIKI RECIPE)

BEETROOT CRESS, TO GARNISH

1. Finely dice onion and garlic.
2. Add oil to a saucepan and heat, then add diced onion and garlic and cook gently until transluscent.
3. Add lamb mince and cook until browned, then add the Madeira and cook for 2 minutes. Season with salt.
4. Add chicken stock and cook for a further 20 minutes. Remove from heat and allow to cool.
5. Finely dice olives and add to lamb mixture.
6. Clarify butter by placing in a microwave for 1 minute (or melting in a saucepan). Once melted, remove the scum from the top using a tablespoon then pour out all the butter fat discarding the milk solids.
7. Take a sheet of filo pastry and brush with the clarified butter (see Note).

Mezedes

8. Place a tablespoon of lamb mixture in the middle of the filo and roll to resemble a 'finger'.

9. Repeat with remaining mixture and pastry sheets.

10. Place fingers on a greased baking tray and cook in preheated oven for 8 minutes at 180°C (350°F) Gas Mark 4.

11. Dust with icing sugar and serve whole with the beetroot tzatziki alongside.

CHEF'S NOTE: In the restaurant we make our own filo pastry but there is nothing wrong with using the ready-made filo pastry from your supermarket. Make sure you keep your filo pastry covered with a damp tea towel or else it will dry out very quickly. This pastry is best used at room temperature.

BEETROOT TZATZIKI
Serves 4

We eat with our eyes and you can taste the beetroot before you put it into your mouth. Like tomato and basil, beetroot and yogurt make an amazing combination.

4 LARGE BEETROOTS

200G (6½OZ) THICK GREEK YOGHURT

½ GARLIC CLOVE, MINCED

ZEST OF 1 ORANGE

JUICE OF 1 LEMON

1. Wrap beetroot individually in foil and bake on a baking tray in a low oven, 120°C (275°F) Gas Mark 1, for 2 hours.

2. Allow to cool, remove from foil and, using a small knife, peel the skin off the beetroot.

3. Dice beetroot into small cubes.

4. In a mixing bowl combine yoghurt, beetroot, garlic, orange zest and lemon juice and mix. Season with salt and serve.

CHEF'S NOTE: Wear disposable gloves when handling beetroot as it will stain your hands.

CRISPY FRIED SCHOOL PRAWNS, OUZO MAYONNAISE

Serves 4

I love this recipe because it represents me: 'Greek-Australian'. The school prawns are fantastic Australian produce and the ouzo mayonnaise reflects my Hellenic background. Use good-quality ouzo—the stuff that you would drink.

200G (6½OZ) SCHOOL PRAWNS (SHRIMP)

50G (2OZ) PLAIN FLOUR

50G (2OZ) OUZO MAYONNAISE (SEE OUZO MAYONNAISE RECIPE)

1 TEASPOON CELERY SALT

LEMON WEDGES, TO SERVE

1. Refrigerate school prawns on paper towel for half an hour to remove any excess liquid (see Note).
2. Toss prawns in the flour and then place in a sieve to remove excess.
3. Deep fry prawns at 180°C (350°F) for 3 minutes, or until golden and crispy.
4. Season with the celery salt and serve immediately with a wedge of lemon.

CHEF'S NOTE: The school prawns that we use at the restaurant come from the Clarence River in NSW; they're a fantastic product, but we need to educate our diners to eat the entire prawn as the flavour is in the head.

Ouzo Mayonnaise

Serves 4

12 GOLDEN SHALLOTS

2 CUPS (500ML/16FL OZ) OUZO (PLOMARI)

3 STAR ANISE

6 EGG YOLKS

4 EGGS

1 TABLESPOON DIJON MUSTARD

¾ TABLESPOON WHITE VINEGAR

4 CUPS (1L, 32FL OZ) OLIVE OIL

1. Slice shallots and place in a saucepan with ouzo and reduce to approximately ¹/₃ cup (85ml/2¾fl oz).
2. Lightly toast star anise in a flat pan until you can smell the aroma and then pound in a mortar and pestle until a powder-like consistency (see Note).
3. Whisk egg yolks, eggs and mustard in an electric mixer on a medium speed until the mixture is white.
4. Add vinegar and continue to whisk for a further 2 minutes.
5. Slowly add the oil until it reaches a thick consistency.
6. Slowly whisk in the reduced ouzo and ground star anise.
7. Place mayonnaise in a dish, ready to serve.

CHEF'S NOTE: If you do not have a mortar and pestle, you can use a coffee grinder instead. To keep your mortar and pestle clean, once a month cover the inside with salt. The salt removes any impurities and bacteria.

Mezedes

PICKLED CABBAGE

Serves 4

This is a great meze to have with beer. Its vinegar and salt taste along with its oily texture is a great combination on a hot day. Please be aware of the long marination time needed. Make sure you keep the cabbage in its brine when serving. It goes very well with fresh, crusty bread.

½ CABBAGE
¼ CUP (60ML/2FL OZ) HONEY
¾ CUP (190ML/6FL OZ) VINEGAR
¼ CUP (60ML/2FL OZ) OLIVE OIL
½ LARGE ZUCCHINI (COURGETTE)
½ STICK CELERY
½ BUNCH CORIANDER (CILANTRO)
RED KAHEL TO GARNISH

1. Roughly cut cabbage, place in a saucepan with a very small amount of water and steam for 7 minutes. Remove from saucepan, drain and allow to cool in a bowl.
2. Mix honey, vinegar and olive oil in another bowl.
3. Finely slice zucchini and celery and add to cabbage. Then pour the honey mixture over the cabbage and marinate for 1 day.
4. Add the chopped coriander and serve.

PICKLED OCTOPUS

Serves 4

This is a true representation of classic and simple Greek cookery. You can't get this wrong or it'll be a disaster! This is a great ouzo meze and lasts for weeks in your fridge.

1KG (2LB) LARGE, CLEANED OCTOPUS

4 GARLIC CLOVES, CRUSHED

½ TABLESPOON THYME, CHOPPED

150ML (5FL OZ) RED WINE VINEGAR

150ML (5FL OZ) OLIVE OIL

½ TEASPOON SMOKED PAPRIKA

1 TABLESPOON GROUND CUMIN

½ TEASPOON FRESHLY GROUND WHITE PEPPER

SALT TO TASTE

CHICKPEA CRESS, TO GARNISH

1. Place octopus in a large saucepan with ¾ cup (200ml/7fl oz) water and simmer, covered, for 1 hour (see Note).
2. Remove octopus and liquid from pan and place in a large bowl, cover with cling film and refrigerate.
3. Once cold, remove octopus from liquid and cut into thin slices at an angle.
4. Take garlic, thyme, red wine vinegar, olive oil, paprika, cumin and add to sliced octopus (see Note). Season with salt and ground white pepper, to taste.

CHEF'S NOTE: When buying octopus ask your fishmonger for 'beaten' octopus as the octopus will be a lot more tender than unbeaten. Also, make sure you peel the skin off the octopus before cooking. Smoked paprika can generally be bought at your local supermarket; if it's the first time you've ever used it, I would suggest to start with a mild paprika (it comes sweet, semi-sweet and hot) until you become accustomed to its taste.

THE PRESS CLUB OUZO FIZZ

Serves 4

If you have never drunk ouzo this is a great cocktail to get your palate used to the flavour. I love this cocktail on a Sunday before lunch; or even accompanying some freshly shucked oysters.

5 CUPS (1250ML/40FL OZ))TANQUERAY GIN
¼ CUP (60ML/2FL OZ) PLOMARI OUZO
½ CUP (100ML/3FL OZ) LEMON JUICE
¼ CUP (60ML/2FL OZ) SUGAR SYRUP
DASH OF EGG WHITE
8 SLITHERS GINGER
SODA WATER TO FINISH

1. Combine the ingredients into 2 cocktail shakers (see Note). Fill each shaker with lots of ice and shake vigorously for approximately 10 seconds (see Note).
2. Strain liquid evenly over 4 cocktail glasses filled with crushed ice.
3. Top with soda water and garnish with ginger chopsticks.

CHEF'S NOTE: To make a sugar syrup, combine equal parts of cold water and sugar in a saucepan. Bring to the boil, or until sugar dissolves.

An American or Boston cocktail shaker can be used. A strainer is not required as all shaken ingredients are poured straight into glass. (Of course, if you only have 1 cocktail shaker, follow the recipe for 1 glass.)

Mezedes

OREKTIKA
Small dishes

'Now that your palate has been teased, your gastric juices are flowing and your appetite is screaming out for more...'

OREKTIKA–SMALL DISHES

Now that your palate has been teased, your gastric juices are flowing and your appetite is screaming out for more, we hit you with our orektika. This is a selection of appetizers designed to bring out the different flavours of Greece all on one plate, creating a harmonious balance between sweet, savoury and sharp. There are scallop loukoumades, where scallops are coated with batter and sit on a bed of taramasalata accompanied by a scattering of salmon roe, topped with drizzles of Attiki honey and candied lemon zest. You will also find soft-shell crab moussaka, where a generous smear of visinada (sour cherry syrup) sits beneath roasted eggplant (aubergine) layered with traditional tzatziki on top of which sits a soft-shelled crab, accompanied by bone marrow.

The orektika at The Press Club can be eaten as an individual appetizer, although trying to choose which one to have may be a difficult task, so we suggest you share a few between you.

OYSTERS KATAIFI, ONION STIFADO, GREEK SALAD SMOOTHIE

Serves 4

Using oysters in this recipe is unorthodox in many ways as kataifi is a traditional Greek dessert that is here being transformed into a savoury dish. It's a bit controversial. However, there's nothing wrong with controversy as long as it works. Some advice, make sure the oyster shells are at room temperature when serving.

12 SHUCKED OYSTERS
250G (8OZ) KATAIFI PASTRY
200G (6½OZ) CLARIFIED BUTTER
ONION STIFADO (SEE ONION STIFADO RECIPE)
VEGETABLE OIL FOR FRYING
1 CUP (250ML/8FL OZ) GREEK SALAD SMOOTHIE (SEE GREEK SALAD SMOOTHIE RECIPE)

1. Remove oysters from their shells. Set shells aside.
2. Brush the kataifi pastry with the clarified butter and wrap neatly around each oyster tightly (see Note). Place in refrigerator until needed.
3. Place 1 tablespoon of warm onion stifado in each oyster shell.
4. Deep fry oysters until just golden at 180°C (350°F).
5. Place on paper towel to remove excess oil. Place oysters back into their shells and serve along with the Greek salad smoothie.

CHEF'S NOTE: Kataifi can be bought at delicatessens. It is made up of thin strands of dough that resemble woolly threads. When working with the threads, cover the ones not being used with a damp cloth, as with filo pastry, as it dries out very quickly. Place oysters on a dry cloth after removing them from their shells to take away excess moisture and stop the kataifi going soggy.

ONION STIFADO

Serves 4

6 GOLDEN SHALLOTS

1 RED ONION, PEELED

2 BROWN ONIONS, PEELED

1 TABLESPOON THYME

3 CLOVES GARLIC

2 CUPS (500ML/16FL OZ) OLIVE OIL

1. Roughly chop shallots and onions (see Note).
2. Place on a roasting tray with the thyme, garlic and oil.
3. Cover with foil and place in a preheated oven, 130°C (250°F) Gas Mark ½ for 2½ hours or until tender. Strain in a fine colander and store until needed.

CHEF'S NOTE: Stifado is traditionally a stew, containing whatever kind of meat you want. Most Greeks use rabbit, with the main ingredient being onions. For this recipe, I have taken the onion idea and incorporated it with oysters instead (see Oysters Kataifi recipe).

Greek Salad Smoothie

Serves 4

This Greek salad smoothie is from my Reserve restaurant repertoire. The smoothie must be powerful in flavour. It's basically like drinking all the fabulous, fresh ingredients that go into a traditional Greek salad. Superb.

2 CUCUMBERS

1 RED ONION, PEELED

250G (8OZ) CHERRY TOMATOES

1 CLOVE GARLIC

1 TABLESPOON FETA

2 TABLESPOONS OLIVE OIL

SALT AND PEPPER, TO TASTE

1. Peel and remove seeds from cucumber and roughly chop onion.
2. Place tomatoes, cucumber, onion, garlic and feta in a food processor and blend for two minutes, or until smooth.
3. Add oil and blend for one minute.
4. Strain through a fine colander and serve.

CHEF'S NOTE: Feta is a white, dry, crumbly cheese made from goat's and cow's milk. The word 'feta' can also mean a 'slice of' something in Greek.

Skordalia Soup, Poached Apple Egg

Serves 4

Let's be totally honest here. I wouldn't expect you to make this recipe at home. This recipe is for chefs, and chefs who have very, very accurate scales. But give it a try!

4 Granny Smith apples
2½ cups (600ml/20fl oz) skordalia soup (see Skordalia Soup recipe)
4 poached apple eggs (see Poached Apple Egg recipe)
Chervil, red kahel and mache to garnish

1. Using a mandolin, slice 1 apple to 2mm ($^1/_{10}$in) thick, avoiding the core (there is no need to peel the apple). Then finely slice to resemble matchsticks (see Note).
2. To finish skordalia soup, bring to the boil and aerate it using a hand blender to make it light and fluffy (see Notes).
3. To serve, scatter apple matchsticks in the bowl, then, very carefully, add 1 poached apple egg on top and finally pour the soup carefully around the poached apple egg (see Note).

CHEF'S NOTE: A mandolin can be bought at any kitchen shop or Chinese food store. It is great for slicing vegetables accurately. Please make sure you use the guard so you don't cut yourself!
I use the word 'aerate' to finish the soup. Pour your hot soup into a stainless steel jug, then using a hand-held blender whisk the soup up and down until you create a frothy layer on top of the soup. This adds both flavour and texture.
Once poached, the apple egg is very sensitive. It can burst with the tiniest amount of friction (bear this in mind in step 3). I mention this because the bursting sensation of the egg on the palate is truly like no other.

Skordalia Soup
Serves 4

Skordalia is that classic Greek purée that you typically eat with baked beans. I have taken that idea and made it thoroughly modern. This is a light, fluffy soup, full of flavour that in turn doesn't detract from the garlic. When I make a soup, I don't complicate it with other vegetables. If it's pumpkin soup, I only use pumpkin. Simple, yet effective. Roasting the garlic in foil removes all its bitterness and nasty, lingering garlic flavour. If you do this, you can guarantee yourself and your guests a nice, sweet garlic soup that doesn't leave a bitter odour and taste on your tongue afterwards.

1 GARLIC HEAD, PUREED

3 GOLDEN SHALLOTS

50G (2OZ) UNSALTED BUTTER

4 CUPS (1L/32FL OZ) CHICKEN STOCK (SEE CHICKEN STOCK STANDARD RECIPE)

½ CUP (125ML/4FL OZ) CREAM

1. Wrap garlic head in foil and bake in a moderate oven, 180°C (350°F) Gas Mark 4 until soft for between 45 minutes to and hour.
2. Let cool at room temperature and then squeeze roasted garlic from its skin (see Note).
3. Slice shallots and in a medium sized pan, gently sweat in butter until translucent.
4. Add garlic purée to shallots and cook gently until well mixed.
5. Pour in the chicken stock and reduce by half to approximately two cups (500ml/16fl oz).
6. Add the cream and bring to a gentle simmer.
7. Remove from the heat and blend in a food processor until smooth.
8. Strain mixture through a fine chinois and season to taste.

CHEF'S NOTE: When squeezing the garlic it's advisable to wear disposable gloves so that you don't retain the pungent aroma of the roasted garlic on your fingertips.

Poached Apple Egg

Serves 4

2 CUPS (500ML/16FL OZ) APPLE JUICE

2½G (¹/₁₀ OZ) CALCIUM CHLORIDE

2G (¹/₁₄ OZ) SODIUM ALGINATE

2 CUPS (500ML/16FL OZ) WATER

1. In a bowl, dissolve the calcium chloride in the water and set aside in the refrigerator for 30 minutes.
2. In a jug, combine apple juice and sodium alginate using a hand-held blender.
3. Measure 1¼ tablespoons of the apple juice solution into a half-round measuring spoon and sub-merge into the calcium chloride solution slowly. Once the juice has been tipped from the spoon, take the spoon out and repeat. Allow the chemical reaction to occur for approximately 5 minutes, or until a skin forms around the apple juice.
4. Once the skin has formed around the juice, remove gently using a tablespoon and place in plain water in the refrigerator until needed (this stops the cooking process).

CHEF'S NOTE: After the alginate solution has been combined with the apple juice, you may need to pour the solution into a cryovac bag and seal it to extract all of the foam (gas) at the surface. The foam affects the calcium chloride solution when being poured in.

Orektika

'I came from the UK to work for George. The boys and girls in The Press Club kitchen are my new family. Like all families, we go through good times and bad. Above all, we stick together as one.'
Ian Burch, Pastry Chef

Scallop Loukoumades

Serves 4

This dish is fun—it goes against everything that's traditional about being Greek. My 'yia yia' yells at me when she sees me serve this dish. It just isn't right as far as she's concerned to put 'loukoumades' batter around scallops. This is the Greek version of tempura.

160G (5½OZ) PLAIN FLOUR

PINCH OF SALT

PINCH OF SUGAR

⅔ CUP (160ML/5FL OZ) LUKEWARM WATER

7G (¼OZ) FRESH YEAST

8 CUPS (2L/64FL OZ) CANOLA OIL (SCALLOPS EXPAND WHEN DEEP FRIED)

12 WHOLE SCALLOPS, ROE ON

50G (2OZ) PLAIN FLOUR, EXTRA

1. Place flour into a mixing bowl and add the salt and sugar.
2. In a jug, whisk the water and yeast together and let stand for 2–3 minutes (see Note).
3. Pour the yeast mixture into the flour and mix until smooth.
4. Cover the bowl tightly with cling film and leave in a warm, dry place to prove (see Note).
5. Heat the oil in a large saucepan to about 180°C (350°F).
6. Lightly dust the scallops in the extra flour. Then coat with the loukoumades batter. Place in the palm of your hand and squeeze from the index finger down straight into the hot oil and fry until golden brown and crispy (see Note).
7. Remove from the oil and season immediately.

TARAMASALATA

Serves 4

½ BROWN ONION, PEELED
70G (2¾OZ) TARAMA PASTE
250G (8OZ) OLIVE OIL POMME PURÉE (SEE OLIVE OIL POMME PURÉE RECIPE)
JUICE OF 1 LEMON
100ML (3FL OZ) SOUR CREAM

1. Roughly chop the onions, place in a food processor and blend until a liquid-like consistency.
2. Add the tarama paste and blend until the ingredients are well combined (see Notes).
3. Add the pomme purée and blend once more, gradually adding the lemon juice, until smooth (see Notes). Add the sour cream and mix well to combine.

CANDIED LEMON ZEST

Serves 4

1 LEMON

3½ CUPS (750ML/24FL OZ) WATER

175G (6OZ) SUGAR

1. Remove the zest from all the lemons with a peeler, then finely slice lengthways (see Note).
2. Place zest in a saucepan and cover with ¾ cup (200ml/7fl oz) of the water and bring to the boil.
3. Once boiling, strain and repeat this process 3 times.
4. Place the remaining cup (250ml/8fl oz) of water and sugar in a saucepan, bring to the boil and allow to cool.
5. Add the zest to the sugar syrup, cover and let stand for 24 hours in refrigerator.
6. Strain. Zest is ready to use.

CHEF'S NOTE: When removing the zest from the lemons, make sure you remove the white pith from the zest because it is very bitter, otherwise you'll end up with a bitter-tasting zest.

LEMON HONEY DRESSING

(Makes 250ml)

¾ CUP (190ML/6FL OZ) ATTIKI HONEY

2 LEMONS

1. Gently warm honey in a small saucepan, and add the zest of both lemons, and the juice of 1 lemon. Stir to combine.
2. Remove from the heat and let stand for up to 3 hours before using.

CHEF'S NOTE: When making the honey dressing, bear in mind that the hotter you let the honey get while warming it, the thicker it'll be when cooling and as a dressing. This will change the texture and flavour when eaten.

71

Textures of the Greek Salad:
Seafood 'Greek Fries', Black Olive Sorbet, Feta Soufflé, Cucumber Salad, Tomato Tea

Serves 4

The Greek salad is such a moreish dish with beautiful, vine-ripened tomatoes, fresh cucumber and olive oil. What more could one ask for? So, we have taken all these elements, broken them down and heightened them. This dish represents the chef in many ways with its thought, technique and skill. The seafood Greek fries are quirky, they remind me of Sunday lunch at home.

200g (6½oz) whitebait

50g (2oz) plain flour

1 litre (1¾pints) canola oil (for deep frying)

salt

4 scoops black olive sorbet (see Black Olive Sorbet recipe)

4 feta soufflés (see Feta Soufflé recipe)

4 portions cucumber salad (see Cucumber Salad recipe)

2 cups (500ml/16fl oz) Tomato Tea (see Tomato Tea recipe)

Red kahel to garnish

1. Toss the whitebait in the flour. Shake off any excess flour and deep fry at 180°C (350°F) until golden and crispy. Remove from fryer and season with salt immediately.
2. Serve salad in individual dishes.

BLACK OLIVE SORBET
Serves 4

4 CUPS (1L/32FL OZ) FULL-CREAM MILK
100G (3½OZ) CASTER SUGAR
300G (10 OZ) GLUCOSE POWDER
200G (6½OZ) PITTED BLACK OLIVES

1. Combine milk, sugar and glucose in a small saucepan and gently heat.
2. Add olives, remove saucepan from the heat and allow to infuse whilst cooling.
3. Once cooled, blend in a food processor until smooth.
4. Place in a Pacojet canister and freeze/churn as required following manufacturer's instructions (see Note).

CHEF'S NOTE: In a few of our recipes for ice-cream and sorbets I know we say to use a Pacojet and I also know that not everyone has one. You can use a household ice-cream machine or even allow to set in the freezer and mix every so often with a fork, however an ice-cream maker is recommended.

Feta Soufflé
Serves 4

2 CUPS (500MLS/16FL OZ) BÉCHAMEL SAUCE (SEE BÉCHAMEL SAUCE STANDARD RECIPE)

300G (10 OZ) DODONI FETA

1 TABLESPOON CORNFLOUR

1 TABLESPOON WATER

WHITES OF 3 EGGS

50G (2OZ) BUTTER, SOFTENED

50G BREAD CRUMBS

1. Heat béchamel in a small saucepan, then add crumbled feta and whisk until smooth.
2. In a small bowl, combine cornflour with the water to make a slurry (see Notes).
3. Add slurry to the béchamel and stir to thicken until it reaches a sauce-like consistency. Allow to cool with a cartouche on top (see Notes).
4. Whisk egg whites to firm peaks, then gently fold into the feta mixture until smooth (see Notes).
5. Brush each soufflé mould thoroughly with the softened butter, brushing upwards. Then dust inside with bread crumbs.
6. Add soufflé mix to each mould, remembering to clean the rim of each mould with the tip of your thumb, to allow it to rise evenly whilst cooking (see Notes).
7. Bake in a preheated moderate oven, 180°C (350°F) Gas Mark 4 for 9 minutes.

CHEF'S NOTE: Don't be afraid of making a soufflé. It's a myth that they're hard to make. Just follow my recipe and also remember to preheat your oven. Once you've folded your egg whites into the feta mixture, try not to over mix it as you will lose all the air at its base.

A slurry is when starch is mixed with liquids (e.g. stock/water).

A cartouche is a circle of buttered greaseproof paper placed over the contents in a dish to retain moisture and prevent a skin forming.

Whisking egg whites to firm peaks means the whites stand up without collapsing, like peaks.

Orektika

CUCUMBER SALAD

Serves 4

4 LEBANESE CUCUMBERS
¼ BUNCH DILL
8 MINT LEAVES
½ LEMON
2 TABLESPOONS OLIVE OIL

1. Wash and cut the cucumbers in half lengthways. With a teaspoon, remove all the seeds then finely slice at an angle.
2. Remove leaves from dill and mint stalks and tear leaves.
3. In a small bowl mix cucumber and herbs and add the juice of ½ lemon and add the olive oil.
4. Season to taste and serve.

'MY RECIPES ARE NOT SET IN STONE, THEY'RE GUIDELINES. COOK FROM THE HEART.'
GEORGE CALOMBARIS

Crispy Soft-Shell Crab Moussaka, Smoked Bone Marrow, Cherry Purée, Traditional Tzatziki

Serves 4

I hate moussaka because that's what people's perceptions are of Greek food. Done correctly it can be beautiful. Done incorrectly, it's a disaster. I've taken the concept of moussaka and made it my own. The cherry purée is a fabulous combination of European sweet and sour. And then there's the addition of smoked bone marrow that turns this dish on its head. Don't be afraid of trying out and mixing together new flavours. This dish works, it's got thought, balance and above all, substance.

2 EGGPLANTS (AUBERGINES)

4 TEASPOONS SALT

¼ CUP (60ML/2FL OZ) OLIVE OIL

4 TABLESPOONS UNSALTED BUTTER

1 TABLESPOON THYME

1 GARLIC CLOVE

4 SOFT-SHELL CRABS, FRESH OR FROZEN

4 TEASPOONS FLOUR, TO DUST

12 PIECES SMOKED BONE MARROW (SEE SMOKED BONE MARROW RECIPE)

80G CHERRY PURÉE (SEE CHERRY PURÉE RECIPE)

4 TABLESPOONS TZATZIKI (SEE TRADITIONAL TZATZIKI RECIPE)

SHISO CRESS, TO GARNISH

1. To prepare the eggplants, cut them in half, score the flesh with a knife and sprinkle with table salt. Leave for 1 hour to release the bitterness, then rinse well and dry.
2. Sear the eggplant flesh side down in hot oil and then bake in a preheated warm oven, 170°C (325°F) Gas Mark 3 for 4 minutes.
3. In a saucepan, heat butter, thyme and garlic until the butter turns light brown and frothy (burre noissett). Add the eggplant slices and coat for 1 minute. Remove and place on absorbent paper towel.
4. To prepare the crabs, remove helmet from the top of the crab then remove the hairy legs that are beneath the helmet. Place on absorbent paper to remove any excess moisture (see Notes).
5. To cook, dust lightly in flour and deep fry until crispy at 180°C (350°F). Once removed from the fryer, immediately season with salt.
6. Place a line of cherry purée along the centre of a serving plate.
7. Place the eggplant on top of the purée and then add a spoonful of tzatziki and then finish with the fried, soft-shell of crab on top.
8. Place 3 pieces of smoked bone marrow around the eggplant.
9. Drizzle with olive oil and garnish with the shiso cress (see Notes on Garnish).

CHERRY PURÉE
Serves 4 (Makes 280g)

200G (6½OZ) CAN SOUR CHERRIES
100G (3½OZ) CASTER SUGAR

1. Place cherries and sugar in a saucepan, bring to the boil, reduce to a simmer until it reaches a jam-like consistency.
2. Remove from the heat and transfer to a food processor and blend until smooth.
3. Strain through a fine colander and let cool before serving.

Smoked Bone Marrow
Serves 4

Ask your butcher to remove the marrow from the beef bone. Before using you must leave the marrow in a bucket of water for 24 hours, or until the marrow turns white and there is no remaining blood.

200G (6½OZ) HICKORY CHIPS

100G (3½OZ) LONG-GRAIN RICE

4 STAR ANISE

2 CINNAMON STICKS

250G (8OZ) BEEF BONE MARROW (BONELESS)

1. In a deep baking tray lined with foil, place the hickory chips, rice, star anise and cinnamon.
2. Place the bone marrow on a cooling rack, spreading it out evenly.
3. Place the tray over a naked flame (barbecue grill or gas stove top) allowing it to smoke.
4. Place the rack of bone marrow over the baking tray and cover both with foil.
5. Keep on the flame for 5 minutes, this allows it to distil and create its initial heat.
6. Remove from flame and let stand, covered, for 1 hour.
7. Remove bone marrow from the rack and heat under a very hot grill to serve.

Traditional Tzatziki
Serves 4

40G (1½OZ) CUCUMBER

200G (6½OZ) THICK GREEK YOGHURT

½ GARLIC CLOVE, CRUSHED

2 TABLESPOONS WHITE VINEGAR

1 TABLESPOON ATTIKI HONEY

1 TEASPOON CAYENNE PEPPER

1. Cut cucumber in half and de-seed with a small teaspoon, then dice.
2. Combine remaining ingredients in a bowl. Stir well and check for seasoning.

'Modern Tzatziki' Cucumber Spaghetti, Yoghurt Raviolo, Grape and Olive Lady's Finger

Serves 4

The Greeks have one of the longest life expectancies in the world. Why? A simple diet. Yoghurt is a staple commodity that's included at the start and can appear throughout a meal. It has always been used in Greek cooking and it also has excellent digestive antibodies. This dish represents all that. I've taken the yoghurt and made it into a raviolo. The cucumber is cut so it looks like spaghetti and the olive lady's finger adds a particular richness to the dish. Make sure you rest the pasta dough before you roll it out and never put salt in your pasta dough as it 'cooks' the yolks. One final tip—salt the water you are going to cook your raviolo in heavily. It should taste like the sea.

4 CUCUMBERS

8 MINT LEAVES

½ BUNCH DILL

1 LEMON

HALF PORTION PASTA DOUGH (SEE PASTA DOUGH STANDARD RECIPE)

4 PORTIONS YOGHURT RAVIOLO (SEE YOGHURT RAVIOLO RECIPE)

4 GRAPE AND OLIVE LADY'S FINGERS (SEE GRAPE AND OLIVE LADY'S FINGER RECIPE)

LEMON WEDGES, TO SERVE

1. Peel the cucumber and push half a cucumber at a time through a Japanese mandolin (see Notes).
2. To make the cucumber salad, place the cucumber 'spaghetti' in a bowl, add the mint, dill and juice of the lemon.
3. Place the grape and olive fingers on a greased baking tray and bake in a moderate 180°C (350°F) Gas Mark 4 oven for 8 minutes. Blanch the raviolo in heavily salted, boiling water for 4½ minutes.
4. Place all ingredients on a serving plate, garnished with lemon slices.

Orektika

YOGHURT RAVIOLO

Serves 4

500G (1LB) THICK GREEK YOGHURT

2 LEMONS, ZESTED

½ BUNCH CHIVES

150G (5OZ) CHICKEN MOUSSE (SEE CHICKEN MOUSSE STANDARD RECIPE)

1 EGG

½ PORTION PASTA DOUGH (SEE NOTES) (SEE PASTA DOUGH STANDARD RECIPE)

1. Combine the yoghurt, lemon zest, finely chopped chives and chicken mousse in a bowl.
2. Check seasoning and allow to stand for 1 hour.
3. Lightly beat the egg and set aside (see Notes).
4. Set pasta machine to lowest setting and gradually roll through pasta dough.
5. Cut pasta dough into 10cm x 10cm (4in x 4in) squares; brush with egg wash and place 1 heaped tablespoon of yoghurt farce in the centre of half the squares (see Notes). Apply another sheet of dough over the stuffing then seal, making sure all air is released. Cut around each piece of raviolo and remove excess dough with a 5cm (2in) cutter (see Notes).
6. To cook, boil in heavily salted water for 4 minutes.

GRAPE AND OLIVE LADY'S FINGER

Serves 4

200G (6½OZ) RAISINS
¼ CUP (60ML/2FL OZ) SHERRY VINEGAR
²⁄₃ CUP (160ML/5FL OZ) RED WINE
½ CUP (125ML/4FL OZ) PORT
8 GREEN PITTED OLIVES
4 SHEETS FILO PASTRY
100G (3½OZ) CLARIFIED BUTTER

1. In a small saucepan combine the raisins, vinegar, wine and port.
2. Cook on a low heat until the raisins have absorbed the liquid and are tender. Place in a food processor and blend until smooth.
3. Finely dice olives and set aside.
4. Lay one sheet filo pastry down and brush with clarified butter. Add raisin purée along the middle and place diced olives on top. Roll the length of the sheet to replicate a long 'finger'. Repeat process with all filling and filo sheets to get four long fingers in total.
5. Place fingers on a greased baking tray and cook in a preheated moderate oven, 180°C (350°F) Gas Mark 4 for 8 minutes.

Orektika

Cyprian Pork Pies, Pine Nut Hommos, Shaved Fennel and Onion Salad

Serves 4

12 PORTIONS CYPRIAN PORK PIES (SEE CYPRIAN PORK PIES RECIPE)

4 TABLESPOONS PINE NUT HOMMOS (SEE PINE NUT HOMMOS RECIPE)

1 RED ONION

1 FENNEL

10 FLAT PARSLEY LEAVES

¼ CUP (60ML/2FL OZ) OLIVE OIL

JUICE OF 1 LEMON

CHICKPEA CRESS, TO GARNISH

1. Deep fry the pork pies until golden and crispy.
2. Place 1 tablespoon pine nut hommos on a plate with pork pies on top.
3. To make the fennel and onion salad, finely slice onion and fennel. Place in a bowl with the parsley, oil and lemon juice and season to taste with salt and pepper. Mix well and place on top of the pork pies to serve. Garnish with chickpea cress.

CYPRIAN PORK PIES

Serves 4

Pastry

150G (5OZ) BURGHAL

3 TABLESPOONS CORNFLOUR

3 TABLESPOONS PLAIN FLOUR

2 CUPS (500ML/16FL OZ) CHICKEN STOCK

(SEE CHICKEN STOCK STANDARD RECIPE)

Stuffing

1 ONION, PEELED

1 GARLIC CLOVE

1 TEASPOON THYME

400G (12½OZ) PORK MINCE (GROUND PORK)

¾ CUP (190ML/6½FL OZ) MADEIRA

4 CUPS (1L/32FL OZ) CHICKEN STOCK

(SEE CHICKEN STOCK STANDARD RECIPE)

2 TABLESPOONS SHERRY VINEGAR

¼ CUP (60ML/2FL OZ) OLIVE OIL

2 TABLESPOONS PINE NUTS

2 TABLESPOONS SULTANAS

1. To make the pastry, place the burghul in a heatproof bowl, then heat chicken stock in a saucepan to boiling point. Pour 1½ cups (400ml/14fl oz) of stock over the burghal Cover and leave to cool. Set remaining stock aside.
2. Once cool, separate burghal grains with a fork, add the sifted flours and a small amount of remaining stock (enough to form a dough), knead until it's the consistency of pastry and let rest.
3. To make the stuffing, dice the onion, crush the garlic and chop the thyme.
4. In a heavy based saucepan, sauté onion, garlic, thyme and mince and continue stirring until mixture browns.
5. Add the Madeira and cook until liquid is reduced by half. Then add the remaining stock and the vinegar and simmer gently until pork is tender and stock has been absorbed.
6. Toast pine nuts in a saucepan with the olive oil until golden. Add toasted pine nuts and sultanas to pork and mix in. Refrigerate until needed.
7. To assemble the pies, take 1 tablespoon pastry and roll into a ball, then press gently to form a patty.
8. Put 1 teaspoon of the mince mixture in the middle of the pastry, then fold both sides together and press firmly to form a semi circle.
9. Deep fry the pork pies until golden and crispy.
10. Serve with shaved fennel salad and the pine nut hoummos.

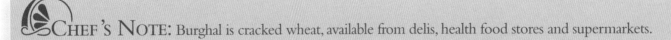

CHEF'S NOTE: Burghal is cracked wheat, available from delis, health food stores and supermarkets.

PINE NUT HOUMMOS

Serves 4 (makes 600g)

3 TABLESPOONS PINE NUTS

¼ CUP (60ML/2FL OZ) OLIVE OIL

1 GARLIC CLOVE, CRUSHED

1 x 250G (8OZ) TIN CHICKPEAS

1½ CUPS (375ML/12FL OZ) CHICKEN STOCK (SEE CHICKEN STOCK STANDARD RECIPE)

1 TEASPOON TAHINI

LEMON JUICE, TO TASTE

SALT, TO TASTE

1. Toast pine nuts in a saucepan with the olive oil until golden.
2. Add the crushed garlic to the pan and continue to cook. Drain and rinse the chickpeas and add to the pan.
3. Add the chicken stock to the pan and reduce by half. Place in a food processor and blend until smooth.
4. Add the tahini, lemon juice and salt, to taste (see Note).

CHEF'S NOTE: Tahini (ground sesame seeds) can be purchased from Mediterranean delis, health food stores and some supermarkets. It is usually eaten during Lent.

Baklava of Baby Squid, Onion Stifado

Serves 4

The argument still continues. Who created the first baklava, the Turks or the Greeks? You know who I'm going to go for, and you know one other thing is certain; you've never eaten this dish before. I'm proud of this dish because it's clever. Make sure you don't boil the squid too rapidly because they will split. The sauce is rich and moreish. Make sure you've got plenty of crusty bread to mop it all up.

2 CUPS (500ML/16FL OZ) CHICKEN STOCK (SEE CHICKEN STOCK STANDARD RECIPE)

150G (5OZ) BUTTER

¾ CUP (190ML/6FL OZ) ATTIKI HONEY

PINCH OF SALT

100G (3½OZ) SLIVERED ALMONDS

100G (3½OZ) WALNUTS

1 TABLESPOON SHERRY VINEGAR

12 BABY SQUID TUBES

4 PORTIONS ONION STIFADO (SEE ONION STIFADO RECIPE)

BEETROOT CRESS TO GARNISH

1. Toast the almonds and walnuts in preheated oven, 160°C (310°F) Gas Mark 2½ until golden brown. Allow to cool then finely dice.
2. In a small saucepan, combine the chicken stock, butter, ⅓ cup (100ml/4fl oz) of the honey and salt. Slowly bring to simmering point and keep warm.
3. In a small saucepan bring remaining honey to the boil, and whisk in the vinegar. Pour this over the nuts and mix well to bind.
4. Place 1 heaped tablespoon of nut mixture inside each tube.
5. Place squid into the stock and heat gently for 5 minutes but do not allow to boil. Drain gently then serve on top of the onion stifado.

Orektika

Sashimi Tuna, Candied Kalamata Olives, Risogalo Foam

Serves 4

This is the Greek version of sushi: rice and raw tuna. I've made the rice pudding recipe and turned it into a foam that's light, aerated and full of flavour. The tuna must be fresh and the candied olives give a great contrast to this dish; they act like wasabi does in a Japanese meal. You can make the candied olives weeks in advance and store them in an airtight container.

500G (1LB) SASHIMI-GRADE TUNA

2 TABLESPOONS OLIVE OIL

PINCH OF SEA SALT FLAKES

4 TABLESPOONS CANDIED KALAMATA OLIVES (SEE SAGANAKI MARTINI RECIPE)

4 PORTIONS RISOGALO FOAM (SEE RISOGALO FOAM RECIPE)

1. Dice tuna into 5mm x 5mm ($\frac{1}{5}$ inch x $\frac{1}{5}$ inch) cubes.
2. Mix diced tuna with olive oil and season with sea salt flakes, place into glass of the ¾ way up.
3. Add risogalo foam on top at the last minute. Place candied olives on the side.

CHEF'S NOTE: Sashimi-grade tuna is the top grade for tuna. It should be rich red in colour and without sinew.

Risogalo Foam
Serves 4

Risogalo is the classic Greek rice pudding recipe. Go down to your local Greek sweet shop and have one, or even two. This will help you understand the rationale behind this dish.

150G (5OZ) BASMATI RICE
1 CINNAMON STICK
2 STAR ANISE
PINCH OF SEA SALT FLAKES
4 CUPS (1L/32FL OZ) MILK

1. In a medium sized saucepan combine all the ingredients and boil for 5 minutes.
2. Strain through a fine colander.
3. Place in a foam canister and gas with 2 soda bulbs (see Note).
4. Allow to cool. Shake well and scrve.

CHEF'S NOTE: Foam canisters and soda bulbs can be bought from good kitchen shops. A soda bulb is a small aluminium bulb filled with carbon dioxide. It's usually used for carbonating home-made soft drinks and soda syphons. It's sometimes more commonly known as an iSi soda syphon and is used for serving drinks.

Cyprian Easter-bread Raviolo, Aphrodite Salad, Almond Vinaigrette

Serves 4

The Greek Orthodox calendar plays a major role in what gets cooked throughout the year. When my 'yia yia' cooks the Cyprian Easter Bread (commonly called the Flaona), you know it's the month of April. People have fasted for Lent and this bread represents the end of the fasting period. I've taken all the ingredients in the bread and made it the filling for raviolo. The Aphrodite Salad accompanies the raviolo. One of the myths of Aphrodite, the Greek goddess of love and beauty, is that everywhere she walked roses would grow. In her memory I've made a delicate and feminine rose-petal salad. Make sure you add the dressing to the salad just before you serve it as the petals wilt quickly.

12 pieces Easter bread raviolo (see Easter Bread Raviolo recipe)
4 portions Aphrodite salad (see Aphrodite Salad recipe)
⅓ cup (80ml/2½fl oz) almond vinaigrette (see Almond Vinaigrette recipe)

1. Place raviolo in boiling, salted water for 4 minutes then drain.
2. Serve on a plate and garnish with the Aphrodite salad and spoon the vinaigrette around the raviolo.

Cyprian Easter-Bread Raviolo

Serves 4

50G (2OZ) MYZITHRA

50G (2OZ) CHEDDAR

100G (3½OZ) HALOUMI

50G (2OZ) FETA

1 LEMON

20G (1OZ) SULTANAS

¼ BUNCH CHIVES

100G (3½OZ) CHICKEN MOUSSE (SEE CHICKEN MOUSSE STANDARD RECIPE)

10G (½OZ) PINE NUTS

½ BUNCH MINT, FINELY CHOPPED

½ PASTA DOUGH RECIPE (SEE PASTA DOUGH STANDARD RECIPE)

1 EGG

1. Finely grate the myzithra, cheddar and haloumi and in a large bowl mix with the feta, lemon zest, sultanas and chopped chives and bind with the chicken mousse (see Notes).
2. Toast the pine nuts in preheated cool–warm oven, 160°C (310°F) Gas Mark 2½ until golden brown. Add to the cheese mixture together with the mint.
3. Roll pasta dough through the pasta machine on its finest setting.
4. Cut pasta dough into 10cm x 10cm (4in x 4in) squares; brush with egg wash and place 1 heaped tablespoon of stuffing in the centre of half the squares (see Notes). Apply another sheet of dough over the stuffing then seal, making sure all air is released. Cut around each piece of raviolo and remove excess dough with a 5cm (2in) cutter (see Notes).
5. To store raviolo, place on a well-floured tray and refrigerate until needed.

CHEF'S NOTE: Myzithra is a by-product of feta cheese. It is hard in texture and very salty so be careful about adding extra salt to a dish when using it. It is available at most Greek delis.
The egg wash we use in this recipe is simply a beaten egg. To egg wash something simply means to stick something together with.

Orektika

Aphrodite Salad

Serves 4

16 ROSE PETALS
1¼ TABLESPOONS OLIVE OIL
RED KAHEL TO GARNISH

1. Mix in the rose petals, red kahel and add the olive oil and toss salad gently to combine (see Notes). Season with salt and serve immediately.

CHEF'S NOTE: Make sure you use edible rose petals. Most roses are edible, but as with all flowers wash them well and avoid any that have been sprayed with chemical pesticides. If in doubt, don't eat them.

Almond Vinaigrette

Serves 4 (Makes 250ml)

50G (2OZ) FLAKED ALMONDS
¾ CUP (190ML/6FL OZ) OLIVE OIL
1 LEMON
1 TABLESPOON SEEDED MUSTARD
SALT, TO TASTE

1. Toast flaked almonds in preheated cool–warm oven, 160°C (310°F) Gas Mark 2½ until golden brown.
2. Mix olive oil and lemon juice with the almonds and seeded mustrad, season to taste with salt and serve immediately.

Orektika

'THERE IS NO SUCH THING AS FRONT OR BACK OF HOUSE. IN OUR RESTAURANT, MY WAITERS AND WAITRESSES ARE TREATED LIKE MY CHEFS—WITH RESPECT. IF I CAN'T RESPECT MY STAFF, HOW DO I RESPECT MYSELF?'
GEORGE CALOMBARIS

Mountain Tea Smoked Chicken Shanks, Tomato Tea Jelly, Ouzo Hollandaise

Serves 4

Greek mountain tea is such a fantastic digestive. It's great to drink at the end of your meal. I've taken the mountain tea leaves and smoked the chicken shanks with them. The tomato jelly is the opposite to everything else in this dish. It's a neutral but very refreshing addition.

12 CHICKEN WINGS
20G (¾OZ) MOUNTAIN TEA (FROM GREEK DELI)
200G (6½OZ) HICKORY CHIPS
3 X 2½G (¹/₁₀ OZ) GELATINE GOLD LEAF SHEETS
1½ CUPS (375ML/12FL OZ) TOMATO TEA JELLY (SEE TOMATO GIN TEA RECIPE)
4 TABLESPOONS OUZO HOLLANDAISE (SEE OUZO HOLLANDAISE RECIPE)
MOUNTAIN TEA TO GARNISH

1. To use only the mini shanks (centre bone of the wing) of chicken wings, using a small knife, scrape the bone towards the knuckle until the bone is exposed to half-way down the shank. Continue this process with all wings and refrigerate if not using straightaway.
2. Mix mountain tea and hickory chips together and place in a deep baking tray lined with foil.
3. Place the shanks on a cooling rack that fits into the lined baking tray. Then over a naked flame on a barbecue grill or gas stove top, allow the contents of the tray to smoke.
4. Cover rack and tray with foil and keep on the flame for 5 minutes.
5. Soak gelatine sheets in iced water until softened.
6. Heat ¼ cup (50ml/2fl oz) tomato tea. Squeeze any water out of the gelatine sheets and dissolve them in the tea.
7. Add the remaining tomato tea to the liquid, pour into a glass dish and refrigerate until set.

Orektika

Ouzo Hollandaise
Serves 4. Makes 200ml

There is no cheat's way to make this hollandaise. Please make it properly. Follow the recipe and don't take any shortcuts. And don't forget to use good quality ouzo.

8 GOLDEN SHALLOTS
¾ CUP (190ML/6FL OZ) OUZO (PLOMARI)
8 EGG YOLKS
1¼ CUPS (300ML/12FL OZ) CLARIFIED BUTTER

1. Finely chop shallots and place in a saucepan with the ouzo and reduce by half. Remove from the heat and allow to cool.
2. Place egg yolks in a bowl and add reduced ouzo. Whisk over a double boiler until it gets to the ribbon stage (see Notes).
3. Slowly whisk in the clarified butter until blended. Season to taste.

CHEF'S NOTE: A double boiler is used to warm or melt chocolate or whip eggs gently. Two saucepans fit together, with one sitting inside the other. The lower pan holds simmering water which gently heats the mixture in the upper pan. You can, of course, use a heatproof mixing bowl that fits across a saucepan holding simmering water.

Ribbon stage means when the eggs are whipped stiffly enough to form ribbons when dropped from the whisk.

OUZO-CURED OCEAN TROUT, SALT AND VINEGAR CHOCOLATE, YOGHURT SORBET

Serves 4

I'm not completely happy with this dish … yet. It's still under the microscope. I love the salt and vinegar chocolate. The idea came to me whilst eating salt and vinegar chips after a block of chocolate. Be open minded when you eat this. The trout is so under worked and fresh, the salt and vinegar chocolate is overworked and the yoghurt sorbet at the end is there to cleanse everything. Produce, as always, is important, so make sure you try to use sustainable produce like line-caught or farmed ocean trout.

250G (8OZ) OCEAN TROUT

400G (12½OZ) SALT

350G (12 OZ) SUGAR

3 STAR ANISE

2 CUPS (500ML/16FL OZ) OUZO

1 PORTION SALT AND VINEGAR CHOCOLATE (SEE SALT AND VINEGAR CHOCOLATE RECIPE)

1 PORTION YOGHURT SORBET (SEE YOGHURT SORBET RECIPE)

EDIBLE PURPLE VIOLET TO GARNISH

1. Divide the trout into four portions.
2. In a medium sized bowl, combine the salt, sugar and star anise.
3. Pour the mixture over the trout.
4. Submerge the trout in the ouzo and refrigerate for 5 hours. This is to cure the fish (see Note).
5. Remove trout from curing mixture, wash gently in a bowl of cool water and dry on paper towels.
6. Serve a piece of trout per person with a little salt and vinegar chocolate and a scoop of yoghurt sorbet alongside.

CHEF'S NOTE: The purpose of curing is to remove the moisture or water from the flesh and to inhibit bacterial growth.

Salt and Vinegar Chocolate

Serves 4. Makes 200g

150MLS (5FL OZ) CREAM

1¼ TABLESPOONS MILK

200G (6½OZ) CHOCOLATE (DARK 72%)

2 TABLESPOONS SHERRY VINEGAR

1 TEASPOON SALT

1. Make a ganache by bringing the cream and milk to simmering point in a small saucepan. Remove from the heat and whisk in the chocolate. Allow to cool to room temperature.
2. Whisk in the vinegar and salt.
3. Refrigerate until required.

Yoghurt Sorbet

Serves 4

½ CUP (125ML/4FL OZ) HONEY

2 CUPS (500G/1LB) THICK GREEK YOGHURT

½ LIME

1. In a medium-sized bowl, whisk the honey into the yoghurt and add the lime juice.
2. Place into an ice-cream machine and churn. Also can be made in a pacojet.

KYRIA
Main Dishes

'...EXPRESSES THE WARM, COMFORTING SIDE
OF GREEK FOOD. IT EMBRACES THE HOMELY
TASTES AND SMELLS OF SLOWLY COOKED LAMB
OR SUCKLING PIG.'

KYRIA—MAIN DISHES

Our list of 'kyria' expresses the warm, comforting side of Greek food. It embraces the homely tastes and smells of slowly cooked lamb or suckling pig.

In every Greek household there is a kyria, the woman of the house. At the end of the day, as much as the man thinks he is the boss, she really is.

For me, the Yoghurt and Mastic Braised Neck of Lamb is close to perfection. This is my recipe. I have not stolen it from anyone.

I love our kyria dishes because they have so much soul in them. There is no bullshit. What you see is what you get. I love seeing customers huddled around a table sharing these dishes and asking for more bread to mop up all the juices on their plates. This should be the 11th Commandment: 'Good food should be concluded by mopping up the plate with bread'. Amen.

Yoghurt and Mastic Braised Neck of Lamb, Olive Oil Pomme Purée

Serves 4

The diamond of Greece in terms of produce is mastic. It comes from the Island of Chios and it's only in season for three months of the year. It is commonly used in sweets and acts as an emulsifier as well as a flavouring. Its flavour is a cross between vanilla and cinnamon. Too much and it can destroy the dish; not enough and it can be non-existent. This dish for me is timeless and represents all food that has soul in it. It reminds me of why I'm a chef. The neck of lamb is an outstanding cut. You can ask your butcher to leave the bone in it. Don't rush this dish, it develops with time. The addition of the yoghurt is what makes it. The yoghurt breaks down with the lamb and turns into a beautiful textured cheese. The potatoes can only be made this way. Don't change my recipe or you'll be disappointed. We don't boil potatoes in water because water dilutes food, and diluted food is like watching a bad movie.

4 TABLESPOONS OIL

4 LAMB NECKS (180G PORTIONS)

8 GOLDEN SHALLOTS

2G ($^1/_{10}$ OZ) MASTIC

6 SPRIGS FRESH THYME

¼ CUP (60ML/2FL OZ) WHITE WINE

1 CLOVE GARLIC, CRUSHED

ZEST OF 1 LEMON

¼ CUP (60ML/2FL OZ) ATTIKI HONEY

12 CUPS (3L/5PT) CHICKEN STOCK (SEE CHICKEN STOCK STANDARD RECIPE)

500G (1LB) THICK GREEK YOGHURT

4 PORTIONS OLIVE OIL POMME PURÉE, TO SERVE (SEE OLIVE OIL POMME PURÉE RECIPE)

CHICKPEA CRESSS TO GARNISH

1. Heat oil in a heavy based frying pan to medium–high heat and sear lamb necks until dark and caramelised.
2. Remove from the pan and place in a deep baking tray.
3. Roughly dice shallots and place in the baking dish with the lamb.
4. Then add the mastic, garlic, thyme, white wine and lemon zest (see Note). Drizzle the honey over and pour on the chicken stock until lamb and vegetables are just covered. Do not pour too much stock in the tray.
5. Finally, spread the yoghurt over the liquid and lamb and place grease proof paper over the yoghurt and cover the whole tray with foil.
7. Place in a preheated oven, 120°C (250°F) Gas Mark ½ and cook for approximately 10 hours, or until tender.
8. Once cooked, take the lamb necks out of the braising tray and keep warm. Strain the liquid through a fine chinois and place in an appropriate sized pan to reduce and create the sauce.
9. Reduce sauce to a pouring consistency and pour over the lamb accompanied with the pomme purée.

CHEF'S NOTE: Mastic is found on trees that grow on the south island of Greece known as Chios. Prepared mastic comes in small granules and can be purchased from most Mediterranean delis. In the early 1990s, the culinary world was swept up with this craze about an ingredient called the truffle . . . Now, the ingredient to use is mastic.

Kyria

Olive Oil Pomme Purée

Serves 4 (Makes 2.5kg)

1KG (2LB) ROCK SALT
3KG (6LB) DESIRÉE POTATOES
200G (6½OZ) BUTTER
¼ CUP (60ML/2FL OZ) OLIVE OIL
¾ CUP (190ML/6FL OZ) MILK

1. Cover the bottom of a baking tray with rock salt and place whole, unpeeled potatoes on the salt.
2. Bake in a preheated cool–warm oven, 160°C (310°F) Gas Mark 2, for approximately 2 hours, or until a skewer passes through potatoes easily.
3. Whilst hot, cut potatoes in half, then pass through a fine colander (orum sieve or tami).
4. In a medium sized pan heat the butter, olive oil and milk and whisk until blended.
5. Add the sieved potato to the pan and whisk until silky and smooth. Season to taste with salt only.

CHEF'S NOTE: Rule number one; never add pepper to pomme purée as the pepper will over power the delicate rich flavour of the potato. Rule number two; do not let the potatoes get cold while you are passing them as they go gluey in consistency. Rule number three; this is the only way to make pomme purée.

Kyria

ROASTED PORK CUTLET, DODONI FETA CRUMBLE, GREEK COFFEE JUS

Serves 4

There is a lot of good and a lot of bad feta out there. You must know what milk is being used, that is the key to a good feta. We use Dodoni feta at The Press Club because it has 70 per cent sheep's milk and 30 per cent goat's milk. We then turn this elegant feta into a crumble. Make sure the pork cutlet has plenty of fat on it. Remember, fat in moderation is okay. Fat is flavour, use it to cook your pork in. Another tip, don't overcook the pork. People say pork should be cooked well-done, I beg to differ. It should still be juicy inside. You can substitute the Greek coffee jus by making a quick Greek coffee butter. Just whip some butter until smooth and then add some Greek coffee to it until you think the flavour is right. Place this on top of the meat just before you serve it and it will add a new dimension to the dish.

4 X 300G (10 OZ) OTWAY PORK RIB-EYE

50G (2OZ) BUTTER

1 TABLESPOON SAGE LEAVES

1 TEASPOON THYME LEAVES

4 PORTIONS DODONI FETA CRUMBLE (SEE DODONI FETA CRUMBLE RECIPE)

¾ CUP (190ML/6FL OZ) GREEK COFFEE JUS (SEE GREEK COFFEE JUS RECIPE)

PINCH OF SALT

RED KAHEL TO GARNISH

1. Season pork rib-eye with salt then seal on the chargrill on either side and then cook to medium (approximately 8 minutes, 4 minutes on each side, in no oil) and allow to rest.
2. Heat the butter, sage, and thyme until it turns golden brown (burre noisette) and add the pork to coat for 30 seconds (see Note).
3. Spoon feta crumble evenly on top of the rib-eye and place under the grill until golden brown.
4. To serve, place pork on a serving plate and drizzle with the Greek coffee jus and red kahel.

Kyria

DODONI FETA CRUMBLE

Serves 4

100G (3½OZ) DODONI FETA

300G (10 OZ) BAKED BEANS (SEE BAKED BEANS STANDARD RECIPE)

¼ RED ONION, PEELED

100G (3½OZ) FRESH BREADCRUMBS

1. Finely diced red onion. Combine with the feta and baked beans in a bowl and mix well.
2. Toss through the breadcrumbs and refrigerate until ready to serve.

GREEK COFFEE JUS

Serves 4 (Makes 1.5l?)

1½ TABLESPOONS SHERRY VINEGAR

30G (1OZ) BROWN SUGAR

15G (½OZ) GREEK COFFEE

1¼ CUPS (300ML/10FL OZ) LAMB JUS (SEE LAMB JUS STANDARD RECIPE)

20G (¾OZ) BUTTER

1. In a small saucepan combine the vinegar and sugar and heat over a low heat.
2. Whisk in the Greek coffee until dissolved and the consistency is smooth (see Note).
3. In a medium saucepan, heat the lamb jus gently.
4. Combine the liquids and finish the sauce by whisking through the butter to thicken and enrich the sauce so that it's smooth and glossy.

Fish-of-the-day 'Greek Style', Fresh Figs, Pickled Fennel, Spiced Capsicum Dip, Zucchini Fritters

Serves 4

At The Press Club all our fish is cooked to order. We have a designated section with a chef who only cooks fish. The fish section is my favourite. It's what I enjoy cooking. Learning how to cook fish takes time.

4 WHOLE BABY SNAPPER

50G (2OZ) BUTTER

1 TABLESPOON LEMON THYME LEAVES

4 FRESH FIGS

4 PIECES PICKLED FENNEL (SEE PICKLED FENNEL RECIPE)

4 TABLESPOONS SPICED CAPSICUM (SWEET PEPPER/BELL PEPPER) DIP (SEE SPICED CAPSICUM DIP RECIPE)

12 PIECES ZUCCHINI (COURGETTE) FRITTERS (SEE ZUCCHINI FRITTERS RECIPE)

1. Read the chef's note first.
2. Once you have cooked the fish to your liking, finish the fish by adding butter and thyme leaves to the frying pan to buerre noisette. Serve immediately.
3. Serve all condiments (figs, fennel, capsicum dip and zucchini fritters) in separate dishes to accompany the fish.

CHEF'S NOTE: In our kitchen, when an order comes in for one of our fish dishes, a pan is placed on the hottest part of the stove and a little bit of vegetable oil is added and heated to reach a slightly smoking stage. It is only at this stage that you place the fish in the pan. If cooking fish with the skin on, be sure to push down on the fillet firmly to create an even colouring for approximately 30 seconds, and then proceed to cook the fish to your liking. We only ever use non-stick frying pans when cooking fish, purely because they are so reliable and are capable of maintaining a consistent heat. Due to the intense heat the fish doesn't stick to the surface of the pan.

Kyria

PICKLED FENNEL

Serves 4

4 WHOLE BABY FENNEL

¾ CUP (190ML/7FL OZ) OLIVE OIL

2½ CUPS (600ML/20FL OZ) WHITE WINE VINEGAR

100ML (3FL OZ) ATTIKI HONEY

1 TEASPOON WHITE PEPPERCORNS

1 BAY LEAF

1. Trim each fennel bulb and steam for 8 minutes, or until just tender.
2. To make the pickling liqueur, combine the oil, vinegar, honey, peppercorns and bay leaf in a bowl and stir to combine.
3. While the fennel is still hot, immerse into the liqueur and allow to marinate overnight.
4. Strain through a fine colander and serve.

ZUCCHINI FRITTERS

Serves 4

1 ZUCCHINI (COURGETTE)

150G (5OZ) PLAIN FLOUR

100G (3½OZ) CORNFLOUR

¾ CUP (190ML/6FL OZ) SODA WATER

½ CUP ICE

FLOUR TO LIGHTLY COAT

1L (1¾ PINTS) CANOLA OIL (FOR FRYING)

1. Top and tail each zucchini, then slice diagonally, approximately 3mm (⅛in) thick.
2. To make the batter, combine the plain flour and cornflour then whisk in the soda water until smooth.
3. Add the ice to keep the batter cold and store in the refrigerator until needed.
4. To serve fritters, lightly coat in the extra flour then dip in the batter and deep fry in the oil until golden brown.

Spiced Capsicum Dip

Serves 4

1 RED CAPSICUM (SWEET PEPPER/BELL PEPPER)

1 LONG RED CHILLI

100G (3½OZ) FETA

200G (6½OZ) THICK GREEK YOGHURT

1. To remove the skin from the capsicum, cook it on a chargrill, skin-side-up, and once well coloured place in a stainless steel bowl and cover with cling film, so it can sweat. When cool enough to handle, de-seed and peel, making sure all skin is removed.
2. Roast the chilli in a preheated fairly hot oven, 200°C (400°F) Gas Mark 6, or until it has coloured and has become tender. When cool enough to handle, de-seed and discard the seeds (see Note).
3. Place the capsicum, chilli and feta in a food processor and blend until smooth.
4. Transfer to a bowl, fold in the yoghurt until well combined and season to taste before serving.

CHEF's NOTE: Be careful removing the seeds, you can wear rubber gloves to do this and make sure not to touch your face after handling the seeds.

Moussaka Cigar, Cauliflower Skordalia, Passionfruit Vinaigrette

Serves 4

In this recipe we show you how to make a vegetarian moussaka filling for the cigar from scratch. However, if you have your own moussaka recipe use the leftovers and you can roll them into a cigar shape instead by following the recipe below. Vegetarian dishes must be interesting. We, as chefs, should put the same emphasis on vegetarians as we do on everyone else. The passionfruit vinaigrette marries so well with the cauliflower skordalia and adds great dimensions to the moussaka cigar that they all have to be served together. Of course try out different flavours and recipes as you like.

Moussaka Cigar
Serves 4

1 ZUCCHINI (COURGETTE)

1 EGGPLANT (AUBERGINE)

½ CAPSICUM (SWEET PEPPER/BELL PEPPER)

1 CLOVE GARLIC

1 SMALL ONION, PEELED

2 TEASPOONS CANOLA OIL

2 TABLESPOONS TOMATO PASTE

¾ CUP (190ML/6FL OZ) WHITE WINE

4 SHEETS FILO PASTRY

½ CUP (125ML/4FL OZ) BÉCHAMEL SAUCE (SEE BÉCHAMEL SAUCE STANDARD RECIPE)

150ML (5FL OZ) CLARIFIED BUTTER

RED KAHEL AND CHERVIL CRESS TO GARNISH

1. Finely dice the zucchini, eggplant, capsicum, garlic and onion.
2. In a medium sized frying pan, sweat onions and garlic then add the eggplant, zucchini and capsicum. Cook on a low–medium heat, and stir occasionally until all ingredients are soft. Then add tomato paste, and mix in thoroughly. Deglaze with the wine. Cook gently, and stir occasionally until all vegetables are soft and tender. (You might need to add a small amount of water to prevent vegetables from burning.)
5. Allow to cool then place in a food processor and blend until smooth.
6. To make the 'cigar', place a thin line of purée along a buttered filo sheet, then place a thin line of béchamel on top. Then roll filo pastry into the shape of a cigar. Repeat with all sheets.
9. Once rolled, brush each cigar with more butter and bake in a preheated moderate oven, 180°C (350°F) Gas Mark 4, for 8 minutes or until golden brown.
10. On a plate, serve cigar with a small amount of cauliflower skordalia alongside and drizzle with the passionfruit vinaigrette.

'I HAVE WORKED FOR GEORGE FOR FOUR YEARS. THERE ARE A COUPLE OF THINGS GEORGE HATES—BEING CALLED CHEF, WHISTLING IN THE KITCHEN AND DULL MOMENTS. CHEFS SIT IN OFFICES. FOR ME IT'S ALL ABOUT THE FOOD'.
JUSTIN WISE, HEAD CHEF

Cauliflower Skordalia

Serves 4 (Makes 750g)

Skordalia is usually flavoured with garlic, but in this recipe we use cauliflower instead. I love cauliflower because it's so white, pure and neutral in flavour.

½ SMALL CAULIFLOWER

250G (8OZ) BUTTER

⅔ CUP (160ML/5FL OZ) MILK

1 TEASPOON SALT

1. Slice the cauliflower very finely.
2. Melt the butter in a saucepan but do not let it colour. Add the cauliflower and cook very gently until it just starts to colour. Add the milk and cook cauliflower until tender.
3. Strain cauliflower briefly through a fine colander, then transfer to a food processor whilst still hot. Purée until smooth. (You may use a little bit of the strained liquid to help the processor blend the cauliflower.)
4. Season with salt and refrigerate until ready to use.

Passionfruit Vinaigrette

Serves 4 (Makes 250ml)

2 FRESH PASSIONFRUIT

50G (2OZ) ICING SUGAR

½ CUP (125ML/4FL OZ) OLIVE OIL

PINCH OF SALT

1. Prepare passionfruit by cutting them in half to remove seeds and pulp. Set aside.
2. To make the vinaigrette, combine the seeds, pulp and icing sugar in a bowl and slowly whisk in the olive oil until blended. Add salt to taste and serve.

ROASTED MEZEDES OF RABBIT, KROKOS MOUSSE, OUZO AND TUNA MAYONNAISE, OUZO-BRAISED LEEKS

Serves 4

You can't make this dish at home! This is a Chef's dish: a dish that contains our ego. The rabbits we use are farmed rabbits. Here in Australia, wild rabbits are not like the wild rabbits in Europe. Our farmed rabbits are fantastic because they're fed properly and the hygiene is world class. Some say the Persians have the best saffron. No comment! We use Krokos (saffron) from Kosani. You don't need to use as much, the flavour is pungent and totally dramatic. If you can't cook this at home, I would take the ideas and translate them into a simple pasta with saffron and braised rabbit. When cooking, you must look outside the box. As I say, recipes aren't set in stone, they are merely guidelines.

2 WHOLE RABBITS (FARMED) (SEE NOTE)

4 VINE LEAVES

200G (6½OZ) KROKOS MOUSSE (SEE KROKOS MOUSSE RECIPE)

4 PIECES CAUL (STOMACH MEMBRANE)

4 SERVINGS OUZO AND TUNA MAYONNAISE (SEE OUZO AND TUNA MAYONNAISE RECIPE)

4 SERVINGS OUZO-BRAISED LEEKS (SEE OUZO-BRAISED LEEKS RECIPE)

ROCKET CRESS TO GARNISH

1. Clean the rabbit, keeping the fillets, tenderloins, kidney, liver and ribs separately as they all have different uses as well as cooking characteristics (see Notes).
2. Lay out a vine leaf and place 1 tenderloin on top, 1 tablespoon of krokos mousse over the loin and roll in the leaf, then wrap it up in a piece of caulfat (see Notes). Refrigerate until required.
3. In a hot saucepan, seal the loin then bake in a 180°C (350°F) Gas Mark 4 oven until firm to touch—depending on the size of the loin, this can be aproximately 4 minutes.
4. Meanwhile, in a separate pan, sear the kidney, liver, belly (shreaded) and ribs in oil until well coloured.
5. Place all parts of the rabbit onto a plate and accompany with the tuna mayonnaise and braised leek.

OUZO AND TUNA MAYONNAISE
Serves 4 (Makes 750ml)

2 GOLDEN SHALLOTS

1 GARLIC CLOVE

2 TABLESPOONS CANOLA OIL

250G (8OZ) TUNA

¼ CUP (60ML/2FL OZ) OUZO (PLOMARI)

¼ CUP (60ML/2FL OZ) TOMATO KETCHUP

1 CUP (250ML/8FL OZ) OLIVE OIL

1. Finely slice the shallots and garlic and sweat in a hot pan with some oil.
2. Dice tuna and add to saucepan and cook until it begins to caramelise.
3. Deglaze with ouzo and cook for 2 minutes.
4. Add tomato ketchup and cook for 3–5 minutes on a low heat.
5. Remove from the stove and while still hot place in a food processor and blend until smooth. While processor is running, slowly pour in the olive oil to form mayonnaise.

Ouzo Braised Leeks

Serves 4

2 LEEKS, LARGE
2 GOLDEN SHALLOTS
¼ CUP (60ML/2FL OZ) OLIVE OIL
⅔ CUP (160ML/5FL OZ) OUZO (PLOMARI)
100G (3½OZ) BUTTER

1. To prepare leeks, cut lengthways and clean thoroughly. Finely dice the shallots.
2. In a medium sized frying pan, heat oil and sweat the leek and shallot together and, once soft, deglaze with the ouzo and finish with the butter and season to taste.

Krokos Mousse

Makes 1kg

800G (1LB/12¼ OZ) CHICKEN BREAST, COOKED
3 EGG WHITES
⅔ CUP (160ML/5 FLOZ) THICKENED CREAM
10 THREADS SAFFRON (KROKOS)
SALT TO TASTE

1. Infuse saffron with cream by placing cream on a very low heat until cream is a bright yellow colour. This should take around 10 minutes, then place in a sealed container in the fridge until cold.
2. Dice the chicken breast, discarding as much sinew as possible, and place in a food processor and blend. While machine is still on, pour in the egg white and continue to blend.
3. Add saffron cream and pulse for 5 seconds, season to taste, then refrigerate.

ZUCCHINI FLOWERS STUFFED WITH HORTA, MELIZANOSALATA, WHITE CHOCOLATE OLIVE OIL

Serves 4

You're probably wondering where I got the idea from for this dish. White chocolate olive oil with eggplant? But just think about it. Chocolate has the characteristics of eggplant in many ways. Smoky, sweet and everlasting on the palate. Use zucchini flowers when they're in season and don't use zucchini flowers that are not locally grown. Always check that the flowers are fresh and have not been sitting in a cool-room for weeks. You can tell freshness from the bottom of the zucchini. If it's dry it means it's been picked a long time ago. The 'melizanosalata' can also be used as a simple dip with fresh crusty bread. Make sure when making the white chocolate olive oil you don't heat the chocolate up too much or it will burn.

1 ONION, PEELED

1 CLOVE GARLIC

150G (5OZ) SILVERBEET

250G (8OZ) SPINACH

150G (5OZ) CHICORY

50G (2OZ) FETA

50G (2OZ) RICOTTA

12 ZUCCHINI (COURGETTE) FLOWERS

100G (3½OZ) PLAIN FLOUR

50G (2OZ) CORNFLOUR

1 CUP (250ML/8FL OZ) SODA WATER

¼ CUP PLAIN FLOUR, EXTRA TO LIGHTLY COAT

1 TEASPOON CANOLA OIL

¼ CUP (60ML/2FL OZ) WHITE CHOCOLATE OLIVE OIL (SEE WHITE CHOCOLATE OLIVE OIL RECIPE)

200G (6½OZ) MELIZANOSALATA (SEE MELIZANOSALATA RECIPE)

RED KAHEL, TO GARNISH

Kyria

1. To make the stuffing, finely slice the onion and garlic and sweat in a medium sized pan; once transcluscent add the silverbeet chicory and spinach and cook until wilted. Strain and refrigerate to cool.
2. Once cool add the feta and ricotta to the mixture and mix well. Season to taste.
3. Place mixture into a piping bag and fill each flower until just full, leaving enough room to be able to twist the tip closed.
4. To make the batter, combine the flour and cornflour then add the soda water gradually to prevent lumps.
5. Dip the stuffed flowers lightly in some plain flour, then coat in the batter and deep fry at 180°C (350°F) until golden brown.
6. Serve with the white chocolate olive oil and melizanosalata.

MELIZANOSALATA
Serves 4 (Makes 500g)

2 EGGPLANTS (AUBERGINES)
1 GARLIC CLOVE, CRUSHED
¼ CUP (60ML/2FL OZ) RED WINE VINEGAR
SALT, TO TASTE

1. Grill whole eggplants, until soft, on a barbecue or an open flame to give them a smokey flavour, until tender.
2. Once cooled, peel eggplant and discard skin.
3. Place eggplant in a food processor with garlic and add the vinegar. Season with salt to taste. Blend until smooth. Place in a paper coffe filter to remove any excess liquid (see Note).

CHEF'S NOTE: You can use either an oil or coffee paper filter bag. If you don't have one you can use a colander lined with a clean chux cloth (J cloth/everyday cleaning towel).

Kyria

White Chocolate Olive Oil

Serves 4 (Makes 250ml/8 fl oz)

200G (6½OZ) WHITE CHOCOLATE
¼ CUP (60ML/2FL OZ) OLIVE OIL

1. In a medium sized bowl melt the chocolate in a double boiler.
2. Whisk in the olive oil until well blended and set aside for use. Remain at room temperature.

'I WANT TO BE IN THE BEST KITCHEN IN MELBOURNE. I GET PUSHED EVERYDAY, AND WHEN I THINK I HAVE DONE IT, THE BAR GETS RAISED HIGHER. I WANT TO BE THE BEST AND THIS IS WHERE I HAVE TO BE TO DO IT.'
PETROS DELLIDIS, APPRENTICE CHEF

Kyria

SYNOTHEFTIKA
Side dishes

'TO SHARE IS TO GIVE, TO GIVE IS TO LOVE.
THESE DISHES ARE TO BE SHARED.'

Salad of Cumin-roasted Beetroot, Pistachio Biscuit, Yoghurt Cheese, Attiki Honey Dressing

Serves 4

¾ cup (190ml/6fl oz) olive oil

50g (2oz) cumin seeds

4 whole beetroots

½ cup (125ml/4fl oz) Attiki honey

4 pistachio biscuits (see Pistachio Biscuit recipe)

4 portions yoghurt cheese (see Yoghurt Cheese recipe)

120 ml (4 fl oz) Attiki honey dressing (see Attiki Honey Dressing recipe)

Beetroot cress, to garnish

1. Place half a cup of the oil and half the cumin seeds in a baking dish.
2. Place beetroot in the dish and drizzle with the rest of the oil, cover the dish with foil.
3. Bake in a preheated moderate oven, 180°C (350°F) Gas Mark 4, for 2 hours, or until a skewer passes through the beetroots easily.
4. Toast the remaining cumin seeds in a preheated moderate oven, 180°C (350°F) Gas Mark 4, until golden brown. Put into a small bowl with the honey.
5. When beetroot are cool, peel off the skin and cut into wedges. Toss with the honey mixture, mix well and serve alongside the biscuits, yoghurt cheese and Attiki honey vinaigrette.

Pistachio Biscuit
Serves 4 (Makes 5 pieces)

125G (4OZ) BUTTER
125G (4OZ) SUGAR
5G (¼OZ) PISTACHIO PASTE
4 EGGS
160G (5½OZ) FLOUR
12G (½OZ) BAKING POWDER
10G (½OZ) PISTACHIO NUTS
250MLS (8FL OZ) CREAM

1. Cream butter and sugar at a high speed in an electric mixer.
2. Add pistachio paste and continue to mix. Add the eggs, one by one, mixing slowly after each has been added, on a low speed.
3. In a separate bowl, mix together the flour and baking powder. Then add the pistachios. Fold flour mixture into the egg mixture. Finally, fold in the cream.
4. Place the mixture into tall moulds lined with baking paper and bake in preheated moderate oven, 180°C (350°F) Gas Mark 4 for 18 minutes.

Yoghurt Cheese
Serves 4 (Makes 16 pieces)

1 BUNCH EACH OF MINT AND PARSLEY
½ BUNCH EACH OF CHERVIL AND CHIVES
1 LEMON
½ CUP (125G/4OZ) THICK GREEK YOGHURT

1. Chop all the herbs very finely.
2. Finely grate the zest of the lemon and add to the chopped herbs.
3. Take 1 teaspoon of the yoghurt and roll into a ball. Place the ball of yoghurt into the herbs and coat evenly. Repeat this process until all the yoghurt is used.

ATTIKI HONEY DRESSING

Serves 4 (Makes 250ml/8fl oz)

¾ CUP (190ML/6FL OZ) ATTIKI HONEY

1 LIME

1 TEASPOON FISH SAUCE

¼ CUP (60ML/2FL OZ) WATER

14 CORIANDER (CILANTRO) LEAVES

50G (2OZ) FLAKED ALMONDS

1. Warm honey gently in a saucepan (see Note).
2. Finely zest and juice the lime. Add the juice, zest and fish sauce to the honey.
3. Thin the mixture by gently whisking the water through.
4. Finely chop the coriander and add to the honey mixture.
5. Toast the almonds in a preheated moderate oven, 180°C (350°F) Gas Mark 4, until golden brown. Add to the honey mixture to serve.

CHEF'S NOTE: Choosing Attiki honey means we have our very own 'liquid gold' at the restaurant. This is by far one of the best honeys I've ever tasted. The bees feed upon thyme leaves during their honey-making process. Once again we're showing the versatility of this product—it can be used in both sweet and savoury cookery. It can be purchased at most Mediterranean delis.

Synotheftika

CLASSIC GREEK SALAD

Serves 4

This is a classic Greek salad and notice one thing: it doesn't mention lettuce. Why not? Because a genuine Greek salad doesn't contain any lettuce. I will also let you in on a little secret of mine. The best part of a Greek salad is all the remaining juices at the bottom of the bowl. Enjoy with crusty bread.

4 Roma tomatoes

1 cucumber

½ red onion

½ turnip

3 tablespoons Dodoni feta

14 Kalamata olives

1 teaspoon dried mountain oregano

1 teaspoon sea salt flakes

⅙ cup (40ml/1½fl oz) olive oil

Red kahel, to garnish

1. Remove the core from the tomatoes and roughly chop.
2. Peel and deseed the cucumber and roughly chop.
3. Using a mandolin, finely slice the onion and turnip into rings
4. In a large bowl mix together the tomato, cucumber, onion, feta, olives and turnip. Season with the oregano and salt. Drizzle with the oil, check seasonings and serve with red kahel to garnish.

CHEF'S NOTE: A mandolin can be bought at any kitchen shop or Chinese food store. It is great for slicing vegetables accurately. Please make sure you use the guard so you don't cut yourself!

Synotheftika

'A DINING ROOM SHOULD LOOK TIMELESS AND
FEEL WARM FOR BOTH LUNCH AND DINNER.
ABOVE ALL, A RESTAURANT SHOULD EMBRACE
THE CHARACTERISTICS OF THE MOST BEAUTIFUL
CREATURE ON EARTH—THE FEMALE.'
ANDREW PHILLPOT, SOMMELIER

BAKLAVA PATATES FOURNOU

Serves 4

This dish might be classified as a side-dish in this book, and it might take a little bit of effort in its preparation, but the result will silence even the harshest critic. Potatoes, like pumpkin, are such beautiful vegetables because they can be worked in with so many different flavours and textures. In this case, the nuts are worked in with onions that have been naturally caramelised and absorbed the flavour of the lamb jus. This, of course, does not detract from the natural flavour and texture of the potato itself.

50G (2OZ) WALNUTS, ROASTED

50G (2OZ) ALMONDS, ROASTED

1 BROWN ONION, FINELY SLICED

100G (3½OZ) BUTTER

⅔ CUP (160ML/5FL OZ) LAMB JUS (SEE LAMB JUS STANDARD RECIPE)

6 DESIRÉE POTATOES

1. Toast almonds and walnuts in 150°C (300°F) Gas Mark 2 oven for 10 minutes or until golden. Once cooled, chop walnuts and almonds finely and set aside.
2. Melt the butter in a large pan. Add the onions and cook over low heat for 10-15 minutes until golden brown, soft and caramelised.
3. Add the lamb jus to the caramelised onions and reduce it by two-thirds on a gentle heat.
4. Peel and finely slice the potatoes.
5. Place a layer of sliced potato in a copper pot, then thinly cover with the caramelised onions and a generous sprinkling of the chopped nuts.
6. Place another layer of potatoes and repeat step 5 four times.
7. Finish with a layer of potato on top.
8. Bake in a preheated cool–warm oven, 160°C (310°F) Gas Mark 2, for approximately 1 hour, or until a skewer passes through the potatoes easily. Serve immediately.

Synotheftika

WHITE BEAN SKORDALIA

Serves 4

200G (6½OZ) WHITE BEANS
¼ CUP (60ML/2FL OZ) WHITE VINEGAR
1 CLOVE GARLIC
½ CUP (125ML/4FL OZ) AIOLI (SEE AIOLI STANDARD RECIPE)
DRIZZEL OF EXTRA VIRGIN OLIVE OIL TO SERVE

1. Cover beans with water and leave, uncovered, overnight to soak (see Note).
2. Strain the beans and put into a large saucepan with 20 cups (8pints) of cold water. Cook gently until tender.
3. Strain beans and purée in a blender with vinegar and garlic. Then fold through the aioli and serve.

CHEF'S NOTE: The reason why the white beans cannot have a lid on them overnight is because they release their natural gases, and leaving a lid on would make them sweat.

Never add salt to a pulse whilst cooking them as the salt rtards the skin of the pulse which makes them crunchy

Synotheftika

GLYKA
Sweets

'WITHIN EVERY GREEK THERE IS A SWEET TOOTH
THAT NEEDS TO BE NOURISHED AT ANY TIME OF
THE DAY...'

GLYKA-SWEETS

Yep, I would have to say, Greeks are different to the rest. We certainly have a different attitude when it comes to glyka. Not wanting to generalise, but often Anglo-Saxon kids are told by their parents that if they eat all their greens they will get some dessert. Within every Greek there is a sweet tooth that needs to be nourished at any time of the day. It could even be 5pm. A small piece of fresh baklava and a Greek coffee hits that craving.

I would not say that our desserts at The Press Club are traditional classics. They are classic ideas given a modern twist. For example, we make the baklava into a soufflé. We have taken the ideas and made them lighter, added texture and a large dollop of creativity. For me, a dessert must be a highlight of a meal. It must seal the deal.

Don't be afraid of the following recipes. Take the ideas and make them your own. Change them if you have to and be prepared for mistakes. I do every day.

Tomato Stifado stuffed with Fruit and Nuts, Cypriot Cinnamon Ice-cream

Serves 4

There is one thing you can't do, and that is to compromise the quality of your tomatoes. The tomatoes must be ripe and full of flavour. Use organically grown tomatoes that have been vine ripened. This dish is challenging too, but how can we expect children to eat interesting things once they're older if parents don't positively experiment with food at the dinner table when they're young?

40 VINE-LEAF ORGANIC CHERRY TOMATOES

3 TABLESPOONS HONEY

75G (3OZ) WALNUTS

150G (5OZ) SPLIT ALMONDS

80G (3OZ) CASTER SUGAR

1 TEASPOON GROUND CINNAMON

160ML (5FL OZ) SHERRY REDUCTION (SEE SHERRY REDUCTION RECIPE)

4 PORTIONS CYPRIOT CINNAMON ICE-CREAM (SEE CYPRIOT CINNAMON ICE-CREAM RECIPE)

1. Score skin of the tomatoes and blanch in boiling water for 10 seconds, then refresh in iced water.
2. Then, gently peel off the skin and slice off the top of each tomato, keeping the stalk intact.
3. Using a small teaspoon, scoop out the inside, turn upside down and place on a paper towel to dry out slightly.
4. Gently heat the honey until just warm.
5. Finely chop the nuts and flavour with sugar and cinnamon.
6. Combine the honey and sugared nuts so that they are covered in the honey and are sticky.
7. Using a teaspoon, fill tomatoes with the nut mixture.
8. Place nut-filled tomatoes in a medium sized saucepan with the reduced sherry and cook at 160°C (310°F) for approximately 7 minutes.
9. Pour a small amount of reduced sherry onto each tomato and keep warm. Serve with the cinnamon ice-cream.

SHERRY REDUCTION
Serves 4 (Makes 400ml/13 fl oz)

300ML (10FL OZ) HONEY

150ML (5FL OZ) SHERRY VINEGAR

1 VANILLA POD, SPLIT AND SCRAPED

½ STAR ANISE

1. In a medium sized saucepan bring the honey to the boil and cook until it's a light caramel colour.
2. Whisk in the sherry vinegar, and add the vanilla pods and star anise. Allow to lightly simmer to enhance the flavour and to reduce slightly (see Note).
3. Allow to cool until ready to use.

CHEF'S NOTE: The more you reduce this glaze, the thicker it will be once it has cooled down, so be careful not to over-reduce it.

Glyka

CYPRIOT CINNAMON ICE-CREAM
Serves 4

A word about ice-cream. In our recipes for ice-cream and sorbets I know we say to use a Pacojet and I also know that not everyone has one. You can use a household ice-cream machine or even allow to set in the freezer and mix every so often with a fork. Making ice-creams and sorbets is not difficult. They're fun and a great way to get your children involved in cooking. Why? Because there is a start and a definite, delicious end. A good tip is to make the ice-cream or sorbet base the day before you put it into your ice-cream machine and store in the refrigerator overnight. It helps the flavour to develop.

1½ CUPS (375ML/12FL OZ) LOW-FAT MILK

4 CYPRIOT CINNAMON STICKS

2 EGG YOLKS

75G (3OZ) CASTER SUGAR

120ML (4FL OZ) CREAM

1. In a medium-sized pan, slowly bring milk and cinnamon sticks to the boil.
2. In a large bowl, whisk egg yolks and sugar together until creamy.
3. Remove cinnamon sticks and add hot milk to egg mixture, whisking continuously. Be careful not to split the eggs.
4. Return mixture to heat in the medium sized pan and continue to heat, stirring constantly until mixture coats the back of a spoon, or if you have a temperature probe, 82°C (180°F). Again, be careful not to overcook the eggs.
5. Let mixture cool and once cold add the cream and place in an ice-cream machine following the manufacturer's instructions.

CHEF'S NOTE: Cypriot cinnamon can be substituted with another. But, I guess I can't compromise my standards when it comes to cinnamon in this recipe.

Glyka

'FOOD IS FAMILY, FAMILY
IS LIFE, LIFE IS EVERYTHING.'
GEORGE CALOMBARIS

FETA AND WATERMELON:
DODONI FETA CHEESECAKE, WATERMELON JELLY, LIME AND YOGHURT SORBET

Serves 4

This dish reminds me of hot summer afternoons at the family beach house with all my cousins where fresh watermelon and wedges of feta were served. If you think the dish is too difficult, just make the feta cheesecake and serve it with fresh watermelon.

280G (9OZ) DODONI GREEK FETA

ZEST OF 2 LEMONS

4 EGG YOLKS

90G (3OZ) CASTER SUGAR

⅓ CUP (80ML/2½OZ) LEMON JUICE

3 SHEETS PRE-SOAKED GOLD-LEAF GELATINE

1¼ CUPS (300ML/12FL OZ) SEMI-WHIPPED CREAM

4 PORTIONS WATERMELON JELLY (SEE WATERMELON JELLY RECIPE)

4 PORTIONS LIME AND YOGHURT SORBET (SEE LIME AND YOGHURT SORBET RECIPE)

1. In an electric mixer on medium–high speed, beat the feta with the lemon zest until soft and creamy in a large bowl. Set aside.
2. Place the yolks and sugar in a bowl over a double boiler in a saucepan until warm, then whisk to a ribbon stage to form a sabayon (see Notes).
3. In a small pan, heat the lemon juice and dissolve leaf gelatine into it (see Notes).
4. Pour the juice into the feta cheese mix and then fold in the sabayon gently.
5. Finish by folding in the whipped cream until well combined.
6. Refrigerate and allow to set before serving.
7. Serve with jelly and sorbet alongside.

Glyka

CHEF'S NOTE: Sabayon is a foamy mixture (a cousin of the light, egg-based Italian dessert zabaglione). It is made by beating egg yolks with a liquid over simmering water, until thickened and increased in volume.

A double boiler is used to warm/melt chocolate gently. Two saucepans fit together, with one sitting inside the other. The lower pan holds simmering water, which gently heats the mixture in the upper pan. You can also use a heatproof mixing bowl that fits across a saucepan holding simmering water. You can now buy gelatine sheets at the local supermarket. Gelatine sheets have three different categories: bronze, silver and gold, which relate to how much heat they can withstand. Gold-leaf gelatine can withstand the highest heat and is the one most commonly available.

WATERMELON JELLY
Serves 4

1½ CUPS (375ML/12FL OZ) WATERMELON JUICE (¼ OF A MEDIUM WATERMELON)
180G GLUCOSE LIQUID (LIGHT CORN SYRUP)
6G (⅕OZ) AGAR AGAR
60G (2OZ) CASTER SUGAR

1. In a saucepan heat the watermelon juice and glucose gently.
2. Mix the agar agar with the sugar (see Notes).
3. Once the juice is just simmering, quickly whisk in the sugar mix and continue to heat.
4. Cook for 2 minutes, stirring continuously.
5. Pass through a fine colander into a mould and allow to set in the refrigerator.

CHEF'S NOTE: Agar agar is a natural gelling agent made from seaweed and it is sometimes used instead of gelatine. It has a very high melting point, and can only dissolve in boiling water. It can be purchased at specialty food stores.

Glucose liquid can also be bought at specialty food stores. Remember, only pick up glucose liquid with wet fingertips.

Lime and Yoghurt Sorbet

Serves 4 (Makes 450ml/14 fl oz)

⅔ cup (160ml/5fl oz) skimmed milk

40g (1½oz) caster sugar

2 limes

25g (30ml/1fl oz) liquid glucose

250g (8oz) thick Greek yoghurt

1. Zest one lime and juice both.
2. In a medium pot bring milk, sugar and lime zest to a light simmer.
3. Remove from heat and cover with cling film and allow to cool at room temperature.
4. Once cooled, whisk in the yoghurt and lime juice. Freeze in a Pacojet or in an ice-cream machine according to manufacturer's instructions.

Glyka

Baklava Soufflé, Smoked Chocolate Ice-cream

Serves 4

There is a rationale behind the following two dishes. Please let me explain. Smoked chocolate and nuts are compatible. The soufflé is not hard to make. Don't be afraid of it. Follow the recipe, it works. The key to a good soufflé is not how high it grows, but how soft it is inside and how moreish. The key to all good cooking is what comes from the heart—it should never be a chore. It should be a passion, the same as an artist has for their canvas.

¾ CUP (190ML/6FL OZ) LOW-FAT MILK

20G (¾OZ) CORNFLOUR

45G (1½OZ) CASTER SUGAR

1 EGG

2 EGG YOLKS

WHITES OF 6 EGGS

100G (3½OZ) CASTER SUGAR

4 PORTIONS SMOKED CHOCOLATE ICE-CREAM (SEE SMOKED CHOCOLATE ICE-CREAM RECIPE)

1. In a medium saucepan, bring milk to the boil. While milk is warming, in a medium bowl mix the cornflour, sugar, eggs and egg yolk together to form a smooth paste.
2. Pour the milk onto the paste and blend together until smooth.
3. Return to the pan, bring to a gentle simmer, whilst whisking continuously for 5–6 minutes.
4. Remove from the heat and pour into a bowl, cover with cling film and allow to cool (see Notes).
5. Once cooled, beat in an electric mixer on medium speed, until smooth.
6. In a medium bowl, whisk the egg whites until foamy and gradually add the sugar, whisking continuously until stiff peaks are formed.
7. Fold ⅓ of the egg white mix into the cooled milk mixture and whisk vigorously, then add the rest and gently fold in.
8. Pour into buttered and sugared soufflé moulds (ramekins) and bake in preheated moderately slow oven, 175°C (350°F) Gas Mark 3 for 13 minutes, or until the soufflé has risen to 2.5cm (1in) above the rim of its mould. Serve immediately.

Glyka

SMOKED CHOCOLATE ICE-CREAM

Serves 4

200G HICKORY CHIPS

140G (5OZ) DARK CHOCOLATE

1½ CUPS (375ML/12FL OZ) FULL-CREAM MILK

2 TABLESPOONS LIQUID GLUCOSE

5 EGG YOLKS

160G (5½OZ) CASTER SUGAR

64G (2OZ) COCOA POWDER

375ML (12FL OZ) DOUBLE CREAM

1. Smoke the chocolate by lining a heavy and lidded pot with foil and placing hickory chips on top. Place chocolate in a stainless steel bowl inside the pot and heat on high to smoke for 30 minutes.
2. Place the milk and glucose in a heavy based pan and heat but do not allow to boil.
3. In an electric mixer, beat together the yolks, sugar and cocoa powder on medium speed.
4. In a large bowl melt the chocolate over a double boiler.
5. Once the milk is heated, pour ⅓ over the yolk mix and beat together, then pour back into the saucepan and cook at 82°C (180°F), stirring continuously with a wooden spoon.
6. Add the melted chocolate and mix well.
7. Pour in the cream and stir, then pass through a fine colander and chill for one day and then freeze in a Pacojet.

ISLAND OF CHIOS MASTIC PANNACOTTA, GREEK DOUGHNUTS

Serves 4

Yes, I know pannacotta is Italian. I guess we're allowed to borrow one thing from their gastronomic repertoire. The key to a good pannacotta is to serve it in a glass so that you don't have to put as much gelatine in it. The pannacotta shouldn't be of a jelly-like consistency. When you touch it with a spoon it should collapse. The Greek doughnuts are my 'yia yia's' recipe.

1¾ CUPS (440ML/14FL OZ) CREAM
⅔CUP (160ML/5FL OZ) MILK
50G (2OZ) SUGAR
5G (¼OZ) MASTIC
2 SHEETS LEAF GELATINE
1 PORTION GREEK DOUGHNUTS (SEE GREEK DOUGHNUTS RECIPE)
1 PORTION MACERATED STRAWBERRIES (SEE MACERATED STRAWBERRIES RECIPE)

1. In a medium sized saucepan, heat cream, milk and sugar together with the mastic on low heat and let simmer for 15 minutes.
2. In a small bowl, soak the gelatine leaves in iced water, until soft.
3. Squeeze and wring out the gelatine and whisk into the cream mixture. Set aside for 1 hour.
4. Strain through a fine colander and pour into moulds. Allow to set in the fridge.
5. Serve alongside Greek Doughnuts and Macerated Strawberries.

Glyka

GREEK DOUGHNUTS
Serves 4 (Makes approx. 20)

160G (5½OZ) PLAIN FLOUR

PINCH EACH OF SALT AND SUGAR

9G (½OZ) FRESH YEAST

⅔ CUP (160ML/5FL OZ) LUKEWARM WATER

1. Place flour, salt and sugar into a large bowl.
2. In a medium bowl dissolve the yeast with the lukewarm water then pour onto the dry ingredients and whisk until smooth. Cover with cling film and leave in a warm place to prove (rise).
3. Preheat deep fryer to 180°C (350°F).
4. Once the dough has doubled in size, using your hands, squeeze golf-size ball doughnuts straight into the deep fryer (see Note). Cook evenly, whilst stirring continuously, until golden brown.
5. Serve and eat immediately. Don't let them go soggy.

CHEF'S NOTE: To squeeze out the Greek doughnuts: using your fingertips, take the amount of batter you need for one doughnut. Flick your wrist and 'snap' the batter into the palm of your hand and with your arm over the deep fryer (from a height) being careful not to burn yourself, gradually make a fist starting with your index finger and then the rest of your fingers, squeeze the batter out with speed so the doughnut forms its shape upon impact in the hot oil. The 'snap' technique comes with practice. Keep unused doughnut batter wrapped and covered to prevent it from drying out.

MACERATED STRAWBERRIES
Makes 4 portions

1 X 250G (8OZ) PUNNET FRESH STRAWBERRIES

100G (3½OZ) ICING SUGAR

175ML (5½ FL OZ) PINK SPARKLING WINE

1. Place all ingredients in a 2 litre (3½ pints) stainless steel bowl, seal tightly with glad wrap.
2. Place bowl of ingredients over a large pot of simmering water for approximately 1 hour until strawberries are soft. Allow to cook before serving.

Passionfruit Tzatziki, Olive Oil Ice–cream, Candied Fennel

Serves 4

One of my favourite fruits is the passionfruit: it's so sweet but it also has a great balance of acidity. The passionfruit represents the Byzantine era when Greek gods would eat roasted meats with fruit. We call this recipe a tzatziki to be quirky. Instead of cucumber we use fennel because of its natural sugars and its cucumber-like texture. Please don't forget, food is textural in many different ways. Vision-impaired people have the best palate when it comes to tasting food. They have an acute sense of smell, taste and texture.

75G (3OZ) ICING SUGAR

300G (10 OZ) THICKENED YOGHURT

100G (3½OZ) PASSIONFRUIT PURÉE

1 PORTION OLIVE OIL ICE–CREAM (SEE OLIVE OIL ICE-CREAM RECIPE)

1 PORTION CANDIED FENNEL (SEE CANDIED FENNEL RECIPE)

1. Lightly whisk sugar, yoghurt and purée together in a medium sized bowl until combined thoroughly (see Note).
2. Place candied fennel in the bottom of a mould and then pour passionfruit mixture over.
2. Allow to set in the refrigerator.

CHEF'S NOTE: Passionfruit purée can be found at most specialty food stores and is a great alternative to fresh passionfruit when it is not available.

Glyka

Olive Oil Ice-cream

Serves 4 (Makes 500g)

I stole this recipe from my mate David who owns Perama restaurant in Sydney. It's a fantastic representation of classic Greek food. Thanks David! That's another thing that the Greeks do well—embrace each other with a generosity of spirit.

1½ cups (375ml/12fl oz) semi-skimmed milk

1 cinnamon stick

4 egg yolks

150g (5oz) caster sugar

250ml (8fl oz) double cream

1/3 cup (80ml/2½fl oz) olive oil

1. In a medium pan heat the milk and cinnamon stick until at a light simmer.
2. Remove from heat, cover with cling film and allow to infuse for at least 2 hours.
3. Whisk the yolks and sugar in a medium sized bowl until pale and creamy. Set aside.
4. Remove the cinnamon from the milk mixture and reheat.
5. Whisk the egg mixture into the pan and stir until the temperature reaches 82°C (180°F), be careful not to overcook the eggs. If you don't have a thermometer, watch the anglaise closely. Once it starts to thicken in consistency it's ready. Take it off the heat immediately because it keeps cooking even when it's taken off the stove.
6. Pass through a fine colander and chill in the refrigerator.
7. In a medium bowl, whip the cream to softs peak and fold into the chilled custard mix, then whisk in the olive oil.
8. Freeze and churn in a Pacojet as necessary or start the ice-cream machine following manufacturer's instructions (see Note).

Chef's Note: In our recipes for ice-cream and sorbets I know we say to use a Pacojet and I also know that not everyone has one. You can use a household ice-cream machine or even allow to set in the freezer and mix every so often with a fork, however an ice-cream maker is recommended.

Glyka

CANDIED FENNEL

Serves 4

1 CUP (250ML/8FL OZ) WATER
200G (6½OZ) CASTER SUGAR
12 BABY FENNELS

1. In a medium-sized pan bring water and sugar to the boil.
2. Trim up baby fennel, but leave whole, then add to the sugar syrup.
2. Bring back to a very light simmer and place a cartouche on top (see Note).
3. Cook until the fennel is tender and slightly candied. Set aside to cool.

CHEF'S NOTE: A cartouche is is a circle of greased baking paper placed on top of a dish to retain moisture and/or to prevent a skin from forming.

Classic Galaktoboureko, Liquorice Ice-cream, Krokos Syrup

Serves 4

The classic 'galaktoboureko' is a simple milk pie.

500ML (16FL OZ) OF SKIM MILK

250G (8OZ) CASTER SUGAR

1 VANILLA POD, SPLIT AND SEEDS REMOVED

2 EGGS

125G (4OZ) FINE SEMOLINA

150G (5OZ) BUTTER

1 PACKET FILO PASTRY SHEETS (16 SHEETS)

4 PORTIONS LIQUORICE ICE-CREAM (SEE LIQUORICE ICE-CREAM RECIPE)

4 PORTIONS KROKOS SYRUP (SEE KROKOS SYRUP RECIPE)

1. Heat milk, sugar and vanilla seeds from 1 pod in a saucepan without boiling. Stir occasionally.
2. Once heated through, add semolina gradually whilst stirring.
3. Stir to a porridge like consistency, remove from heat and stir in the butter and eggs.
4. Line and grease a 28 x 23 x 8cm (11 x 9 x 3 inch) deep tray.
5. Line the bottom of the tray with 8 sheets of filo pastry, brushing each sheet with clarified butter as you add them.
6. Pour in mixture evenly on top of filo and finish with 8 more buttered sheets of filo pastry on top of the mixture.
7. Bake at 160°C (325°F) Gas Mark 3 until golden brown, approximately 40 minutes.
8. Whilst still hot pour half of the cold saffron syrup onto the Galaktoboureko and allow to absorb.

LIQUORICE ICE-CREAM
Serves 4

This is the dish for me. It's on the menu at The Press Club and I don't think I'll ever take it off. Why? Because I'm obsessed with liquorice. My pastry chef knows that whenever I'm in his kitchen with my head in his freezer, I'm usually eating the liquorice ice-cream. There's one thing I know, you either love liquorice or you hate it. Liquorice and saffron make a great combination.

1½ CUPS (375ML/12FL OZ) LOW-FAT MILK

170G (5½OZ) LIQUORICE STICKS, DICED

2 EGG YOLKS

75G (3OZ) CASTER SUGAR

120ML (4FL OZ) CREAM

1. Place the milk and liquorice into a heavy based saucepan and heat but do not allow to boil. Leave pan on the stove until the liquorice melts.
2. Whisk egg yolks and sugar in a large bowl until combined.
3. Pour ⅓ of the milk over the egg mixture.
4. Heat remaining milk to 82°C (180°F), stirring continuously. Then pass through a fine colander.
5. Add the cream, mix it in well and place in a Pacojet or ice-cream machine and follow manufacturer's instructions (see Note).

CHEF'S NOTE: In a few of our recipes for ice-cream and sorbets I know we say to use a Pacojet and I also know that not everyone has one. You can use a household ice-cream machine or even allow to set in the freezer and mix every so often with a fork, however an ice-cream maker is recommended.

KROKOS SYRUP

Serves 4 (Makes 400ml/12½fl oz)

200G (6½OZ) CASTER SUGAR
¾ CUP (190ML/6FL OZ) WATER
8 SAFFRON (KROKOS) THREADS

1. In a small saucepan, bring the sugar and water to the boil and simmer lightly until reduced by half, approximately 12 minutes. Remove from the heat and add the saffron and cover with cling film and allow to cool.
2. Once cooled, pass through a fine colander, and store in an airtight container in the fridge.

CHEF'S NOTE: I claim saffron as a Greek product. It was first cultivated in Kozani in the 17th century, and is the world's most expensive spice. However, don't let the price deter you, a little bit of saffron goes a long way. Krokos Kozanis Saffron can be found in all Mediterranean delis.

CHOCOLATE RISOGALO, MILK SORBET

Serves 4

This is what being a chef is all about. It's about being able to respect a classic dish but then tweak it and raise it to another level.

¾ CUP (190ML/6FL OZ) LOW-FAT MILK

5G (¼OZ) UNSALTED BUTTER

20G (¾OZ) ARBORIO RICE

1 TEASPOON ATTIKI HONEY

1½ TABLESPOONS HAZELNUT COMPOUND

ZEST OF 1 ORANGE

4 PORTIONS MILK SORBET (SEE MILK SORBET RECIPE)

1. Heat the milk in a heavy based pan until hot.
2. Heat the butter in another medium sized pan, add the rice and stir until it has absorbed the butter.
3. Add the milk to the rice in 4 stages, so the rice can absorb the milk gradually whilst cooking on a low–medium heat, stirring continuously to prevent it from sticking (see Note).
4. Add the honey, hazelnut compound and orange zest and mix in well.
5. Cover, chill and store accordingly. Serve accompanied with the sorbet.

CHEF'S NOTE: Arborio rice is a medium-grain, superfine, pearly rice that is grown in northern Italy. It is available at your local supermarket. Hazelnut compound is a highly concentrated hazelnut flavouring which you can buy from a food specialty store.

Glyka

Milk Sorbet
Serves 4 (Makes 500ml)

This sorbet is not only refreshing and light on the tongue, but also acts as a great digestive.

¾ cup (100ml/7fl oz) low-fat milk
30g (1 oz) liquid glucose
100g (3½oz) caster sugar

1. Place all the ingredients into a medium sized pan and heat gently until the glucose has dissolved.
2. Place in an ice-cream machine and follow the manufacturer's instructions.

'I am a young Greek Australian and proud of it. Finally, a modern Greek restaurant that we are all proud of. Greek is the word!'
Theo Paraskevas, Apprentice Chef

Glyka

Ice Powder Galaktoboureko,
Pistachio Foam,
Candied Pumpkin Seeds

Serves 4

I don't expect you to make this dish at home but give it a go. We've taken the galaktoboureko idea and really turned it on its head. Make the candied pumpkin seeds first.

2¼ CUPS (560ML/17FL OZ) LOW-FAT MILK

½ CUP (125ML/4FL OZ) WATER

40G (1½OZ) CASTER SUGAR

1 TEASPOON NUTMEG

1 EGG YOLK

1 EGG

4 PORTIONS PISTACHIO FOAM (SEE PISTACHIO FOAM RECIPE)

4 PORTIONS CANDIED PUMPKIN SEEDS (SEE CANDIED PUMPKIN SEEDS RECIPE)

EDIBLE FLOWERS TO GARNISH

1. In a heavy-based saucepan, bring the milk, water, sugar and nutmeg to the boil.
2. Mix the egg yolk with the egg in a large bowl.
3. Pour ⅓ of the hot milk mixture onto the eggs, stirring continuously, then return egg mixture to the saucepan with the remaining milk mixture.
4. Heat to 85°C (185°F) over medium heat until it coats the back of the spoon and remove from stove.
5. Pass mixture through a fine colander and allow to cool.
6. Freeze mixture in a rectangular container in the freezer and, using a fork, break down the ice crystals every 45 minutes, or until a frozen powder is formed.
7. Serve with the foam and pumpkin seeds alongside.

Pistachio Foam

Serves 4 (Makes 500g)

1 CUP (250ML/8FL OZ) MILK
20G (¾OZ) PISTACHIO PASTE
6 EGG YOLKS
125G (4½OZ) CASTER SUGAR
250ML (8FL OZ) DOUBLE CREAM

1. Pour the milk and pistachio paste into a saucepan and heat gently (see Notes).
2. Meanwhile, place the yolks and sugar in a food processor and with the egg-whisk attachment, whisk to a light ribbon stage (see Notes).
3. Remove from the machine into a large bowl and set aside.
4. Pour the milk mixture over the egg-yolk mix and blend together with a wooden spoon, stirring continuously.
5. In a saucepan heat the egg-yolk mixture and cook to 82°C (180°F), until it coats the back of a spoon stirring continuously.
6. Add the cream and pass through a fine colander then allow to cool.
7. Once cooled, serve using an espuma (foam) gun or scoop lightly with a spoon.

CHEF'S NOTE: Pistachio paste can be found at most specialty food stores. This really is a fantastic product, not only because of its beautiful green colour and its lovely smell but also it tastes really natural. It's a great substitute for when you don't need that nutty texture.

Ribbon stage means when the eggs are whipped stiffly enough to form ribbons when dropped from the whisk.

CANDIED PUMPKIN SEEDS
Serves 4

I love pumpkin seeds. They remind me of going to the soccer with my dad.

150G (5OZ) PUMPKIN SEEDS
½ TEASPOON CARAWAY SEEDS
100G (3½OZ) CASTER SUGAR

1. Lightly roast the pumpkin and caraway seeds in 180°C (350°F) Gas mark 4 oven for approximately 8-10 minutes and allow to cool.
2. Mix seeds together in a bowl with the sugar and spread onto a baking tray.
3. Dry the mix out in a very low oven, 90°C (194°F) Gas Mark ⅓, for 8 hours.

'WE ALL WEAR BROWN APRONS IN OUR KITCHEN. WHY? BECAUSE WE ARE ALL EQUAL. THERE ARE NO EGOS IN OUR KITCHEN. IF THEY COME, WE GET RID OF THEM VERY QUICKLY. AT THE END OF THE DAY IT'S ALL ABOUT THE FOOD.' TRAVIS McAULEY, SOUS CHEF

Glyka

STANDARD
Recipes

Aioli

Makes 1kg (2lb)

6 EGG YOLKS

1 TABLESPOON LEMON JUICE

2 TABLESPOONS WHITE VINEGAR

1 TEASPOON DIJON MUSTARD

1 LITRE (1¾ PINTS) VEGETABLE OIL

200G (6½OZ) OLIVE OIL POMME PUREE (SEE OLIVE OIL POMME PUREE RECIPE)

1 CLOVE GARLIC, CRUSHED

PINCH OF SALT

1. Whisk egg yolks, lemon juice, vinegar and mustard together.
2. Slowly add oil whilst continually whisking to emulsify.
3. Add crushed garlic and warm pomme puree.
4. Pass through a chinois to retain a smooth consistency.

Baked Beans

Makes 2kg (4lb)

This standard recipe is also a great dish on its own. Grab a bowl of this, some crusty bread and you're in heaven.

1KG (2LB) CANNELLINI BEANS

2 CARROTS, PEELED

4 CELERY STICKS

2 BROWN ONIONS, PEELED

4 GARLIC CLOVES

¾ CUP (190ML/6FL OZ) TOMATO KETCHUP

4 CUPS (1L/32FL OZ) TOMATO PURÉE

1¼ CUPS (300ML/10FL OZ) SHERRY VINEGAR

4 CUPS (1L/32FL OZ) CHICKEN STOCK (SEE CHICKEN STOCK STANDARD RECIPE)

1. Soak cannellini beans overnight covered in water. Do not cover with a lid.
2. Very finely dice carrots, celery, onions and garlic.
3. Heat oil in a medium sized pan and sweat vegetables over a low heat until translucent.
3. Add tomato ketchup, purée, sherry vinegar and chicken stock and bring to a simmer.
4. Add strained beans to the pot and cook for 5 hours, or until beans have absorbed the stock flavours.

Standard

BAKLAVA

Serves 4

Syrup

300ML (10FL OZ) HONEY

¾ CUP (190ML/6FL OZ) WATER

100G (3½OZ) CASTER SUGAR

2 CINNAMON STICKS

2 TEASPOONS LIME ZEST

3 CLOVES

Nut Filling

300G (10 OZ) BLANCHED SPLIT ALMONDS

100G (3½OZ) WALNUT HALVES

125G (4OZ) PISTACHIO NUTS

125G (4OZ) CASTER SUGAR

2 TEASPOONS GROUND CINNAMON

200G (6½OZ) UNSALTED BUTTER

300G (10 OZ) FILO PASTRY

1. To make the syrup, combine all ingredients in a saucepan and bring to the boil.
2. Reduce to a simmer and cook for 10 minutes, strain and allow to cool.
3. To make the nut filling, blitz nuts, sugar and cinnamon together in a blender until fine.
4. Place seven sheets of filo pastry in a tray, brushing each sheet with clarified butter as you add them.
5. Spread half the nut filling on top of the pastry and place a sheet of filo on top.
6. Press down to gain an even surface. Spread the rest of the nut filling on top.
7. Apply another seven sheets of filo pastry brushed with clarified butter remembering to press down to eliminate the air bubbles.
8. Cut portions into diamonds whilst still in the tray and uncooked. Bake at 160°C (325°F) Gas Mark 3 for approximately 15 minutes until golden.
9. When cooked and still hot, pour cold syrup over the baklava so it can be absorbed.
10. Allow to cool at room temperature.

Standard

BÉCHAMEL SAUCE

Serves 4 (makes 600ml)

2 CUPS (500ML/16FL OZ) FULL CREAM MILK

1 SPRIG THYME

1 SPRIG ROSEMARY

1 BAY LEAF

½ GARLIC CLOVE

2 ONIONS, ROUGHLY CHOPPED

50G (2OZ) BUTTER

50G (2OZ) FLOUR

PINCH OF SALT

1. In a small saucepan, infuse the milk with the herbs, garlic and the roughly chopped onion on a moderate heat.
2. In another saucepan make a roux by melting the butter then adding the flour, stirring continuously, until it starts to thicken (see Notes).
3. Once the milk has infused with the herbs for about 15 minutes, strain it and reheat gently on low heat.
4. Add the roux to the infused milk whisking continuously until it thickens and coats the back of a spoon. Season with salt to taste
5. If not using immediately, add a cartouche (see Notes).

CHEF'S NOTE: A roux is when starch is preheated separately in fat such as flour in butter or oil. A cartouche is a circle of buttered greaseproof paper placed over the liquid contents in a dish to retain moisture and prevent a skin forming.

CHICKEN MOUSSE

Makes 1kg (2lb)

800G (1LB, 12¼ OZ) CHICKEN BREAST
WHITES OF 3 EGGS
⅔ CUP (160ML/5FL OZ) THICKENED CREAM
A PINCH OF SALT

1. Dice chicken breast, discarding as much sinew as possible, and place in a food processor and blend. Whilst the machine is still on, pour in the egg whites and continue to blend. Add salt (see Note)
2. Add cream and pulse for 5 seconds, and store in an airtight container.

CHEF'S NOTE: A good idea is to place your food processor bowl in the freezer prior to blending up the chicken. This will help with the mousse not splitting. Salt is important in the mousse as it brings together the protien in the chicken.

CHICKEN STOCK

Makes 40 cups (10L/16 pt)

10KG (20LB) CHICKEN BONES

2KG CHICKEN WINGS

3 BROWN ONIONS, PEELED

3 CELERY STICKS, PEELED

4 CARROTS, PEELED

1 HEAD OF GARLIC

3 BAY LEAVES

1 BUNCH THYME

10 WHITE PEPPERCORNS

1. Roast chicken bones and wings in a preheated hot oven, 200°C (400°F) Gas Mark 6, for 45 minutes or until golden brown. Deglaze tray with a cup of water to remove pan juices (see Note).
2. Place roasted bones into a large, heavy based pan, with pan juices.
3. Chop onions, celery, carrots, peppercorns, bay leaves, thyme and garlic into rough pieces and place in the pot with the roasted bones, leave vegetables quite whole.
4. Cover with cold water and gently simmer for 3 hours.
5. Allow to cool and refrigerate or freeze as needed.

CHEF'S NOTE: Chicken wings are great in chicken stocks as they have amazing flavour, they are the most flavoursome part of the chicken.

Standard

LAMB JUS

Makes 6 cups (1.5l/48fl oz)

4KG (8LB) LAMB NECK BONES

1KG (2LB) CHICKEN WINGS

3 CARROTS, PEELED

2 CELERY STICKS

2 BROWN ONIONS, PEELED

1 HEAD GARLIC

⅔ CUP (160ML/5FL OZ) MADEIRA

½ CUP (125ML/4FL OZ) SHERRY VINEGAR

¾ CUP (190ML/6FL OZ) WHITE WINE

½ BUNCH THYME

3 BAY LEAVES

2 ROSEMARY SPRIGS

10 WHITE PEPPERCORNS

32 CUPS (8L/14PT) CHICKEN STOCK (SEE CHICKEN STOCK STANDARD RECIPE)

1. Place neck bones and chicken wings on trays and roast in a preheated hot oven, 220°C (425°F) Gas Mark 7, for 40 minutes, or until dark brown.
2. Roughly chop the carrots, celery, onion and garlic and fry on medium heat in a large, heavy based frying pan until golden brown.
3. Add the roasted lamb bones, chicken wings and the Madeira, vinegar and wine to the pan and then reduce liquid to a glaze.
4. Add the thyme, bay leaves, rosemary, peppercorns and chicken stock and gently simmer for 3 hours or until flavour develops.
5. Strain through a fine chinois into another saucepan and reduce to a pouring consistency. Once reduced pass through cheese cloth 7 times to remove any impurities.

CHEF'S NOTE: The key to a good sauce is a great stock. Always skim the stock as it is developing flavour. Never boil and make it with love.

Standard

PASTA DOUGH

Makes 500g (1lb)

500G (1LB) PLAIN FLOUR OR DOUBLE ZERO FLOUR

3 EGGS

3 EGG YOLKS

1 TABLESPOON OLIVE OIL

1. Put flour in a food processor and pulse for 20 seconds (see Note).
2. Add whole eggs and egg yolks and pulse until mixture resembles breadcrumbs.
3. Add the oil and pulse for a further 5 seconds.
4. Remove mixture and knead into a ball and wrap in cling film and allow to rest for 2 hours before use.

CHEF'S NOTE: Never add salt to a pasta dough recipe as it draws out the moisture making the dough dry and difficult to roll out.

The egg whites of the whole eggs are included in a pasta dough to enhance the elasticity of the dough.

A NOTE ON GARNISH

All chefs use garnish to finish their dishes. We often use a variety of coloured leaves that add a fine texture. These are the different types of cress, sprouts and fresh herbs. Finishing a dish with a herb or a cress just elevates the dish and softens it as well. Do not go overboard. At the end of the day the garnish is not the king. You can always substitute cresses with picked soft fresh herbs such as tarragon, chervil and dill. Just make sure the flavour of the herb actually goes with the dish you are serving.

Shiso and diakon cress are available from Asian grocers. Red kahel, beetroot, rocket and chickpea cress are available from select herb growers. Rose petals are also used, but make sure these are edible rose petals bought from a food provider.

A NOTE ON HELLENIC WINE

Knowing the parts of Greece where I came from, fills me with such pride and joy I almost burst at the seams. I learnt a very long time ago to honour the land of my ancestors, but to also be grateful for where I am. As a young woman in Greece I stood in vineyards with peculiar indigenous grape varieties like assyrtiko, agiorgitiko, xynomauvro, roditis, liatiko, lagorthi–the list goes on.

I learnt to say these words and taste their fragrances like a history novel. I saw their plights and their wars through their terror and likened the idea of their survival to that of a Hellene–if this were true these grapes would thunder freedom.

The timing of the The Press Club coincided with a few smart Greek wine distributors importing some of the finer wines of Greece. Producers like Gaia, Antonopoulos, Kir-yianni and Boutaris where amongst the first to arrive on these shores. Finally we are drinking respectful and sometimes amazing Greek wines which show how versatile these varietals are. Unfortunately, the only issue I have ever encountered with these wines is their difficulty in pronunciation–my long Greek surname has never been pronounced properly either. I still manage to exist.

Angie Giannakodakis
Restaurant Manager

205

INDEX